St.Mary's Anglican Church

Portage la Prairie, Manitoba

Births, Marriages and Burials

1856-1883

© 2016

Gail Morin

Source: St. Marys Anglican Church, Portage La Prairie, Manitoba, Baptisms, Marriages, Burials, 1855-1883, transcribed by Clarence Kipling, Calgary, Alberta. A copy of the handwritten original may be found at the Glenbow Archives, Calgary, Alberta.

Special Recognition: Geoff Burtonshaw

Adams, Ann Elizabeth
> B-137, Ann Elizabeth Adams, baptized 26 May 1862, daughter of George and Mary Adams of High Bluff. (page 18)

Adams, James Wilson
> B-87, James Wilson Adams, baptized 16 December 1860, son of George and Mary Adams. (page 11)

Adams, John Robert
> B-288, John Robert Adams, baptized 23 June 1867, son of George and Mary Adams, St. Margaret. (page 36)

Adams, Lydia
> B-206, Lydia Adams, baptized 1 February 1864, daughter of George and Mary Adams of High Bluff. (page 26)

Adams, Maria
> B-89, Maria Adams, baptized 8 January 1861, daughter of George and Nancy Adams. (page 12)

Adams, Sarah Jane
> B-354, Sarah Jane Adams, baptized 13 November 1870, daughter of George and Mary Adams of Portage la Prairie. (page 45)

Albright, Georgina
> See George Garrioch and Georgina Albright

Alexander, Charles
> B-307, Charles Alexander, baptized 19 January 1868, son of John and Christianna Alexander, St. Marys. (page 39)

Anderson, Abel
> B-75, Abel Anderson, baptized 27 May 1860, son of Thomas and Fanny Anderson. (page 10)

Anderson, Albert
> B-25, Albert Anderson, baptized 18 January 1856, son of John and Christiana Anderson. (page 4)

Anderson, Ann
> See Charles Whitford and Ann Anderson

Anderson, Benjamin

B-134, Benjamin Anderson, baptized 20 March 1862, son of Henry and Sophia Anderson. (page 17)

Anderson, Betsy

B-283, Betsy Anderson, baptized 3 March 1867, daughter of Thomas and Fanny Anderson, St.Margaret. (page 36)

Anderson, Caroline

S-57, Caroline Anderson, of La Prairie, age 15, buried 22 November 1866. (page 8)

Anderson, Catherine

B-213, Catherine Anderson (adopted), baptized 6 March 1864, daughter of Thomas and Catherine Anderson of Portage la Prairie. (page 27)

Anderson, Catherine

S-35, Catherine Anderson, of Portage la Prairie, age 9 months, buried 19 March 1864. (page 5)

Anderson, Catherine

See Basil Moosoo and Catherine Anderson

Anderson, Charles

B-139, Charles Anderson, baptized 2 June 1862, son of Thomas and Fanny Anderson of High Bluff. (page 18)

Anderson, Charles

B-353, Charles Anderson, baptized 19 October 1870, son of Charles T. and Maria Anderson of Westbourne. (page 45)

Anderson, Charles Thomas and Maria Cook

M-8, Charles Thomas Anderson, age 20, of Laprairie, son of John Anderson, married 10 August 1859, Maria Cook, age 18, daughter of William Cook, by William Cochran, Witnesses: Joseph Alexander Turner and William Erasmus. (page 4)

Anderson, Charles Thomas

B-37, Charles Thomas Anderson, baptized 6 September 1871, son of John and Hannah Anderson of Laprairie. (page 46)

Anderson, Cornelius

B-133, Cornelius Anderson, baptized 16 March 1862, son of John and Christiana Anderson. (page 17)

Anderson, Edward James
B-414, Edward James Anderson, baptized 19 July 1874, son of Alexander and Mary Anderson of Laprairie. (page 52)

Anderson, Eliza
See Andrew Tate and Eliza Anderson

Anderson, Elizabeth
B-42, Elizabeth Anderson, baptized 6 June 1858, daughter of John and Christiana Anderson. (page 6)

Anderson, Elizabeth
S-12, Elizabeth Anderson, of Portage la Prairie, age 20 years, buried 30 August 1858. (page 2)

Anderson, Elizabeth
See Joseph Howse and Elizabeth Anderson

Anderson, Flora
S-2, Flora Anderson, of Portage la Prairie, age 1 year and 4 months, buried 7 June 1856. (page 2)

Anderson, Fredrick H.
B-575, Fredrick H. Anderson, baptized 8 July 1883, son of Archibald and Eliza Anderson of Portage la Prairie. (page 72)

Anderson, Hannah Bella
S-183, Hanna Bella Anderson, of Portage la Prairie, age 9 months, buried 14 March 1882. (page 23)

Anderson, Harriet
B-113, Harriet Anderson, baptized 22 September 1862, daughter of Charles and Ann Anderson of High Bluff. (page 15)

Anderson, Henry
B-36, Henry Anderson, baptized 27 Sep 1857, son of Thomas and Elizabeth Anderson. (page 5)

Anderson, Henry
S-97, Henry Anderson, of St.Margaret, age 40 years, buried 28 September 1873. (page 13)

Anderson, James

B-48, James Anderson, baptized 5 April 1859, son of Henry and Sophia Anderson. (page 6)

Anderson, Jane

See Francis Whitford and Jane Anderson

Anderson, Jemima

B-136, Jemima Anderson, baptized 11 May 1862, daughter of James and Fanny Anderson of High Bluff. (page 17)

Anderson, John and Christiana Whitford

M-_, John Anderson, married 20 May 1857 Christiana Whitford at the home of John Anderson, Portage la Prairie, by Thomas Cochrane, Witnesses: John Anderson and Thomas Anderson. (page _)

Anderson, John and Ada Amanda Mair

M-73, John Anderson, age 26, of Westbourne, son of Thomas W. Anderson, married 9 January 1874, Ada Amanda Mair, age 20, daughter of Holmes Mair, by Henry George, Witness: Alexander Anderson. (page 37)

Anderson, John Henry and Mary Halcrow

M-57, John Henry Anderson, age 19, of St. Marys, son of David Anderson, married 20 July 1870, Mary Halcrow, age 18, of St. Marys, daughter of David Halcrow, by Henry George, Witnesess: James Henderson and Thomas Corrigal. (page 29)

Anderson, John James

B-222, John James Anderson, baptized 9 May 1864, son of James and Fanny Anderson of High Bluff. (page 28)

Anderson, John Michel and Hannah Halcrow

M-58, John Michel Anderson, age 18, of St. Marys, son of Thomas Anderson, married 3 August 1870, Hannah Halcrow, age 15, of St. Marys, daughter of David Halcrow, by Henry Geroge. (page 29)

Anderson, John Peter

B-205, John Peter Anderson, baptized 19 January 1864, son of John and Christiana Anderson. (page 26)

Anderson, Joseph

B-26, Joseph Anderson, baptized 19 February 1857, son of Henry and Sophia Anderson. (page 4)

Anderson, Julia

B-361, Julia Anderson, baptized 30 April 1871, daughter of Peter and Letitia Anderson of Laprairie. (page 46)

Anderson, Lydia

B-312, Lydia Anderson, baptized 7 June 1868, daughter of Peter and Letitia Anderson, St. Marys. (page 39)

Anderson, Margaret

B-174, Margaret Anderson, baptized 31 May 1863, daughter of Robert and Elizabeth Anderson. (page 22)

Anderson, Maria

See William Pocha and Maria Anderson

Anderson, Mary Ann

B-156, Mary Ann Anderson, baptized 25 December 1862, daughter of Charles and Marie Anderson of High Bluff. (page 20)

Anderson, Mary Ann

B-278, Mary Ann Anderson, baptized 28 October 1866, daughter of Peter and Letitia Anderson of Laprairie. (page 35)

Anderson, Mary

B-73, Mary Anderson, baptized 1 May 1860, daughter of James and Fanny Anderson. (page 10)

Anderson, Maurice Charles

B-11, Maurice Charles Anderson, baptized 31 May 1874, son of Peter and Letitia Anderson of Laprairie. (page 52)

Anderson, Nancy

B-389, Nancy Anderson, baptized 23 June 1872, daughter of Thomas and Fanny Anderson of Laprairie. (page 49)

Anderson, Patrick

B-40, Patrick Anderson, baptized 16 May 1858, son of James Francis Anderson and Fanny Gill. (page 5)

Anderson, Robert and Elizabeth Kip

M-25, Robert Anderson, age 20, of Poplar Bluff, son of John Anderson, married 24 March 1863, Elizabeth Kip, age 21, of Poplar Bluff, daughter of Donald Kip, by William Cochrane, Witnesses: David Sandison and Mary Sandison. (page 13)

Anderson, Robert

B-21, Robert Anderson, baptized 31 August 1856, son of James Anderson and Fanny Gill. (page 3)

Anderson, Robina Jane

B-211, Robina Jane Anderson, baptized 25 February 1864, daughter of Charles and Ann Anderson of High Bluff. (page 27)

Anderson, Sarah Helena

See Peter Prince and Sarah Helena Anderson

Anderson, Thomas and Fanny Pocha

M-10, Thomas Anderson, age 26, widower, of Portage la Prairie, son of Thomas Anderson, married 7 September 1859, Fanny Pocha, age 22, daughter of [Joseph Pocha], by William Cochran, Witnesses: Joseph Alexander Turner and William Erasmus. (page 5)

Anderson, Thomas and Elizabeth Desmarais

M-1, Thomas Anderson of LaPrairie, son of Thomas Anderson, married 3 April 1856, Elizabeth Desmarais of same place, daughter of Baptiste Desmarais, by Hellyer, Witnesses: Robert Inkster. (page 1)

Anderson, Thomas

B-71, Thomas Anderson, baptized 5 March 1860 (Heathen parents) (page 9)

Anderson, William

B-360, William Anderson, baptized 21 March 1871, son of John Henry and Mary Anderson of Laprairie. (page 45)

Anderson, William Henry

B-104, William Henry Anderson, baptized 16 July 1861, son of Charles and Marie Anderson, of Poplar Point. (page 13)

Anderson, William

S-77, William Anderson, of Portage la Prairie, age 14 days, buried 2 April 1871. (page 10)

Andreson, Catherine

B-210, Catherine Anderson, baptized 23 February 1864, daughter of Charles and Maria Anderson of High Bluff. (page 27)

Armstong, Martha: See Joseph Glenn and Martha Armstrong

Asham, Ann Margaret

B-271, Ann Margaret Asham, baptized 19 July 1866, daughter of James and Caroline Asham of Coleston. (page 34)

Asham, Catherine Alice

B-303, Catherine Alice Asham, baptized 24 December 1867, daughter of James and Caroline Asham, St. Marys. (page 38)

Asham, Catherine Alice

B-336, Catherine Alice Asham, baptized 18 March 1870, daughter of James and Caroline Asham. (page 42)

Asham, James and Caroline Corrigal

M-16, James Asham, age _, of Westbourne, son of Charles Asham, married 29 August 1861, Caroline Corrigal, age 19, of Westbourne, daughter of James Corrigal, by Thomas Cochrane, Witness: Joseph A. Turner. (page 8)

Asham, Sarah Jane

B-374, Sarah Jane Asham, baptized 11 February 1872, daughter of James and Caroline Asham of Laprairie. (page 47)

Atchinson, John and Catherine Cruckshanks

M-101, John Atchinson, age 26, of Portage, son of William Atchinson, married 27 June 1882, Catherine Cruckshanks, age 25 of Portage, daughter of James Cruckshanks, by A. C. Fortin. (page 51)

Ballenden, Robert William

B-343, Robert William Ballenden, baptized 26 May 1870, son of Catherine Ballenden. (page 43)

Balls, Herbert

B-576, Herbert Balls, baptized 15 July 1883, son of Thomas William and Amy Balls of Portage la Prairie. (page 72)

Baptiste, Samuel

S-3, Samuel Baptiste, of Portage la Prairie, age 12 years, buried 20 May 1857. (page 1)

Bartlett, Wilder and Margaret Walker

M-70, Wilder Bartlet, age 24, of St. Marys, son of Philander Bartlett, married 7 December 1871, Mary Walker, age 23, of St. Marys, daughter of John Walker, by Henry George, Witness: Hugh Walker and Thomas Anderson. (page 33)

Bartlett, Wilder

S-87, Wilder Bartlett, of Portage la Prairie, age 29 years, buried 27 April 1872. (page 11)

Bates, George Frederick Adolph

B-412, George Frederick Adolph Bates, baptized 21 June 1874, son of George and Clara Bates of Laprairie. (page 52)

Bates, Gertrude Adelaide

B-472, Gertrude Adelaide Bates, baptized 15 September 1878, daughter of George and Clara Bates of Portage la Prairie. (page 59)

Bates, John George and Clara Bird

M-70, John George Bates, age 20 of Portage la Prairie, married 17 February 1873, Clara Bird, age 18 of Portage la Prairie, daughter of Frederick Bird, by Henry George, Witness: Flora Garrioch. (page 35)

Bates, Mary Frances Ann

B-441, Mary Frances Ann Bates, baptized 15 June 1876, daughter of George and Clara Bates of Laprairie. (page 56)

Beads, Mary

See Magnus Whitford and Mary Beads

Bird, Adelaide Harriet

B-232, Adelaide Harriet Bird, baptized 18 December 1864, daughter of Frederick and Ann Bird. (page 29)

Bird, Adelaide Harriet

S-47, Adelaide Harriet Bird of Portage la Prairie, age 11 months, buried 27 October 1865. (page 6)

Bird, Catherine

B-72, Catherine Bird, baptized 22 April 1860, daughter of Frederic Adolphus and Anne Bird. (page 9)

Bird, Catherine

See George F. S. Garden and Catherine Bird

Bird, Charles and Ann Hallett

M-27, Charles Bird, of Red River, son of Joseph Bird, married 30 June 1863, Ann Hallett, of Poplar Point, by Thomas Cochrane, Witnesses: George Bird, James Johnson, and Jane Hallett. (page 14)

Bird, Charles Frederick

B-275, Charles Frederick Bird, baptized 18 September 1866, son of Frederick and Ann Bird of Laprairie. (page 275)

Bird, Clara

B-5, Clara Bird, baptized 11 May 1856, daughter of Frederick and Anne Bird of Portage la Prairie. (page 1)

Bird, Clara

See John George Bates and Clara Bird

Bird, Emma Margaret

S-163, Emma Margaret Bird, of Westbourn, age 4 years 4 months, buried 16 August 1880. (page 21)

Bird, Henry George

B-319, Henry George Bird, baptized 23 December 1868, son of Frederick and Ann Bird, St. Marys, La Prairie. (page 40)

Bird, Isabella

See Michel Desmarais and Isabella Bird

Bird, John

S-86, John Bird, of Portage la Prairie, age 12 years, buried 9 February 1872. (page 11)

Bird, Mabel Mary

S-171, Mabel Mary Bird, of Portage la Prairie, age 7 months 9 days, buried 12 January 1881. (page 22)

Bird, Mabel May

B-504, Mabel May Bird, baptized 8 August 1880, daughter of William and Harriet Bird of Westbourne. (page 63)

Bird, Maria

B-138, Maria Bird, baptized 2 June 1862, daughter of Frederick and Ann Bird. (page 18)

Blair, John and Annie Giles

M-105, John Blair, age 33, of Shoal River, son of John Blair and Mary, married 30 May 1883, Annie Giles, age 19, of Shoal River, daughter of Alfred Giles and Sarah, by A. C. Fortin. (page 53)

Bourne, Beatrice Eleanor

B-559, Beatrice Eleanor Bourne, born 24 November 1882, daughter of George and Catherine Bourne of Portage la Prairie. (page 70)

Brown, Curtis James

B-190, Curtis James Brown, baptized October 1863, son of Peter and Mary Ann Brown of Poplar Point. (page 24)

Bruce, John James

B-183, John James Bruce, baptized 23 August 1863, son of James and Elizabeth (Bird) Bruce of Poplar Point. (page 23)

Bruce, Mary Ann

B-435, Mary Ann Bruce, baptized 9 January 1876, daughter of Benjamin and Elizabeth Bruce of Poplar Point. (page 55)

Bruce, Mary Jane

B-215, Mary Jane Bruce, baptized 7 March 1864, daughter of James and Elizabeth Bruce of Poplar Point. (page 27)

Bruce, Mary Josephine

B-392, Mary Josephine Bruce, baptized 13 October 1872, daughter of Patrick and Elizabeth Bruce of Fairford, Catechist. (page 49)

Bruce, Patrick and Elizabeth Garrioch

M-53, Patrick Bruce, age 22, School master, of St.Johns, son of James Bruce, married 6 April 1870, Elizabeth Garrioch, age 21, of St. Marys, daughter of John Garrioch, by Henry George, Witnesses: William Bird, Donald Bruce, and Mary Garrioch. (page 27)

Buchanan, Amelia Margaret Jane

B-480, Amelia Margaret Jane Buchanan, baptized 10 May 1879, daughter of Joseph and Jane Buchanan. (page 60)

Buchanan, Andrew

B-479, Andrew Buchanan, baptized 10 May 1879, son of Joseph and Jane Buchanan. (page 60)

Buchanan, Joseph and Mary Curtis

M-84, Joseph Buchanan, age 33, of Portage la Prairie, son of Joseph Buchanan, married 13 February 1878, Mary Curtis, age 17, of Portage la Prairie, daughter of Charles Curtis, by Henry George, Witnesses: John McKenney and Sarah Curtis. (page 43)

Buchanan, Joseph Curtis
B-498, Joseph Curtis Buchanan, baptized 30 May 1880, son of Joseph and Mary Buchanan of Portage la Prairie. (page 63)

Buchanan, Margaret
B-450, Margaret Buchanan, baptized 1 February 1877, daughter of George and Charlotte Buchanan of Portage la Prairie. (page 57)

Buchanan, Pierce
B-578, Pierce Buchanan, baptized 10 August 1883, son of Joseph and Mary Buchanan of Portage la Prairie. (page 73)

Buchanan, Victoria
B-541, Victoria Buchanan, born 17 April 1882, baptized 15 May 1882, daughter of Joseph and Mary Buchanan of Portage la Prairie. (page 68)

Buchanan, Victoria
S-185, Victoria Buchanan, of Portage la Prairie, age 3 months, buried 23 July 1882. (page 24)

Buchanan, William
B-478, William Buchanan, baptized 10 May 1879, son of Joseph and Jane Buchanan. (page 60)

Burnell, Colin Hambya
B-506, Colin Hamlya Burnell, baptized 17 December 1880, son of Harvey and Jessie Burnell of Portage la Prairie. (page 64)

Burns, Alexander Robert
B-561, Alexander Robert Burns, born 15 February 1851, baptized 4 March 1883 [no parents named]. (page 71)

Burns, Violet Gertrude
B-562, Violet Gertrude Burns, born 19 February 1883, daughter of Alexander Robert and Emma Burns of Portage la Prairie, barber. (page 71)

Burr, Estelle
B-323, Estelle Burr, baptized 27 January 1869, daughter of Frederick and Sarah Burr, St. Marys, La Prairie. (page 41)

Burr, Eugene
B-322, Eugene Burr, baptized 27 January 1869, son of Frederick and Sarah Burr, St. Marys, La Prairie. (page 41)

Byers, Mabel Grant

B-532, Mable Grant Byers, born 5 September 1881, baptized 15 December 1881, daughter of William and Isabelle Byers. (page 67)

Byers, Mary

See Samuel Charles Higginson and Mary Byers

Byers, William and Isabel Dorothy Smith

M-89, William D. Byers, age 26, of Oakland, son of Richard D. Byers, married 25 December 1878, Isabel Dorothy Smith, age 30, of Oakland, daughter of John Smith, by Henry George. (page 45)

Byers, William Herbert

B-497, William Herbert Byers, baptized 20 April 1880, son of William and Isabelle Byers. (page 63)

Cadot, Pierre and Catherine Desmarais

M-30, Pierre Cadot, age 19, of Laprairie, son of Joseph Cadot, married 26 January 1864, Catherine Desmarais, age 15, of Laprairie, daughter of Charles Desmarais, Witnesses: James Johnston and John Corrigal. (page 15)

Cameron, Elizabeth Ann

B-112, Elizabeth Ann Cameron, baptized 22 September 1861, daughter of Thomas and Elizabeth Cameron, of High Bluff. (page 14)

Campbell, Maggie L.

B-572, Maggie L. Campbell, baptized 24 June 1883, daughter of Duncan Fraser and Euphemia Campbell. (page 72)

Carpenter, Samuel and Julia Nelson

M-102, Samuel Carpenter, age 21, of Portage, son of Noah Carpenter and Elizabeth, married 30 December 1882, Julia Nelson, age 22 of Portage, daughter of Henry Nelson and Annie, by A. C. Fortin. (page 52)

Carrie, Grace

See John Diehl and Grace Carrie

Cavanaugh, Catherine

See Francis Scarrow and Catherine Cavanaugh

Cavanaugh, Michael Thomas

B-491, Michel Thomas Cavanaugh, baptized 3 January 1880, son of Dennis and Elizabeth Cavanaugh. (page 62)

Chambers, Gertrude Florence Ethel

B-556, Gertrude Florence Ethel Chambers, born 15 August 1881, daughter of Charles and Mary R. Chambers of Gladstone, Manitoba. (page 70)

Chambers, Mary Edith

B-582, Mary Edith Chambers, baptized 16 September 1883, daughter of John and Mary R. Chambers. (page 73)

Charles, Sara Ann

S-176, Sarah Ann Charles, of Portage la Prairie, age 8 years 8 months, buried 22 June 1881. (page 22)

Clark, Stewart and Lizzie Thompson

M-109, Stewart Clark, age 22, of Portage, son of Edward Clark, married 6 November 1883, Lizzie Thompson, age 21, of Portage, daughter of James Thompson, by A. C. Fortin, Witnesses: James Thompson. (page 55)

Cleaver, James

B-579, James Cleaver, baptized 11 August 1883, son of William and Sarah Cleaver of Portage la Prairie. (page 73)

Cleaver, Richard

S-189, Richard Cleaver, of Portage la Prairie, age 75 years, buried 22 November 1882. (page) 24

Conniff, Wellington and Nellie Davis

B-106, Wellington Conniff, age 36, of Winnipeg, son of James A. Conniff, married 21 January 1883, Nellie Davis, age 22, of Winnipeg, by A. C. Fortin, Witnesses: P. Davis and J. Davis. (page 54)

Cook, Eleonora

B-382, Elenora Cook, baptized 12 May 1872, daughter of William Lyman and Mary Cook. (page 48)

Cook, Elizabeth Jane

See Alexander Whitford and Elizabeth Jane Cook

Cook, Maria

See Charles Thomas Anderson and Maria Cook

Corbett, Owen William
B-242, Owen William Corbett, baptized 21 May 1865, son of Rev. G. Owen and Abigail Corbett missionary of Headingley. (page 31)

Corrigal, Alexy
S-103, Alexy Corrigal, wife of John Corrigal, of Portage la Prairie, age 26 years, buried 27 August 1874. (page 13)

Corrigal, Alice
B-397, Alice Corrigal, baptized 4 May 1873, daughter of Thomas and Ann Elizabeth Corrigal of Laprairie. (page 50)

Corrigal, Caroline
B-244, Caroline Corrigal, baptized 28 May 1865, daughter of Peter Corrigal and Elizabeth Desmarais of Laprairie. (page 31)

Corrigal, Caroline
See James Asham and Caroline Corrigal

Corrigal, Catherine Mary
B-409, Catherine Mary Corrigal, baptized 19 April 1874, daughter of John and __ Corrigal of Laprairie. (page 52)

Corrigal, Christie
B-314, Christie Corrigal, baptized 19 June 1868, daughter of John and Alexie Corrigal, St. Marys. (page 40)

Corrigal, Christie
S-67, Christie Corrigal, of Portage la Prairie, age 5 days, buried 20 June 1868. (page 9)

Corrigal, Fanny
See Charles Cummings and Fanny Corrigal

Corrigal, Hugh Matheson
B-366, Hugh Matheson Corrigal, baptized 20 August 1871, son of John and Alexie Corrigal of Laprairie. (page 46)

Corrigal, James
B-466, James Corrigal, baptized 28 May 1878, son of Flora Corrigal of Portage la Prairie. (page 59)

Corrigal, James Franklin

B-465, James Franklin Corrigal, baptized 17 February 1878, son of Henry and Martha Corrigal, Hotel Keeper. (page 59)

Corrigal, James

S-104, James Corrigal, of Portage la Prairie, age __, buried 31 October 1874. (page 13)

Corrigal, James

S-140, James Corrigal, of Portage la Prairie, age 9 months, buried 28 June 1878. (page 18)

Corrigal, John and Alexy Matheson

M-44, John Corrigal, of Portage la Prairie, son of James Corrigal, married 18 July 1867, Alexy Matheson, of Portage la Prairie, daughter of Hugh Matheson, by Henry George, Witnesses: Nancy Corrigal and Gavin Garrioch. (page 22)

Corrigal, John Robert

S-147, John Robert Corrigal, of Portage la Prairie, age 6 months, buried 2 April 1879. (page 19)

Corrigal, Joseph and Susan Moffat

M-78, Joseph Corrigal, age 24, of Portage la Prairie, son of James Corrigal, married 21 September 1875, Susan Moffat, age 19, of Portage la Prairie, daughter of James Moffat, by Henry George, Witness: Flora Corrigal. (page 40)

Corrigal, Nancy

See Hiram Jacquish and Nancy Corrigal

Corrigal, Roderick James

B-330, Roderick James Corrigal, baptized 28 August 1869, son of John and Alexie Corrigal, La Prairie. (page 42)

Corrigal, Roderick

S-82, Roderick Corrigal, of Portage la Prairie, age 14 years, buried 22 July 1871. (page 11)

Corrigal, Thomas and Ann Elizabeth Hodgson

M-59, Thomas Corrigal, age 20, of St. Marys, son of James Corrigal, married 13 October 1870, Ann Elizabeth Hodgson, age 18, of St. Marys, daughter of William Hodgson, by Henry George, Witnesses: Charles Cummings, Louisa Smith, Fanny Corrigal, and Joseph Corrigal. (page 30)

Corrigal, William James

B-429, William James Corrigal, baptized 4 July 1875, son of Thomas and Elizabeth Corrigal of Laprairie. (page 54)

Cowan, James N.
S-131, James N. Cowan, of Portage la Prairie, age 20 years, buried 6 August 1877. (page 17)

Cowan, Joseph
B-379, Joseph Cowan, baptized 2 April 1872, son of Dr. James and Janet Cowan of Laprairie. (page 48)

Cowan, Joseph
S-130, Joseph Cowan, of Portage la Prairie, age 6 years, buried 27 August 1877. (page 17)

Cruckshanks, Catherine
See John Atchinson and Catherine Cruckshanks

Cummings, Ann Harriet
B-329, Ann Harriet Cummings, baptized 30 May 1869, daughter of Malcolm and Margaret Cummings, La Prairie. (page 329)

Cummings, Catherine
B-287, Catherine Cummings, baptized 19 May 1867, daughter of Malcolm and Margaret Cummings, La Prairie. (page 36)

Cummings, Charles and Fanny Corrigal
M-60, Charles Cummings, age 26, of St. Marys, son of Charles Cummings, married 25 January 1871, Fanny Corrigal, age 25, of St. Marys, daughter of James Corrigal, by Henry George, Witnesses: Albert Scott and Mary Garrioch. (page 30)

Cummings, Curtis James
B-406, Curtis James Cummings, baptized 15 March 1874, son of Charles and Fanny Cummings of Laprairie. (page 51)

Cummings, Cuthbert
S-81, Cuthbert Cummings, of Portage la Prairie, age 18 years, buried 15 July 1871. (page 11)

Cummings, Flora Ann
B-373, Flora Ann Cummings, baptized 24 December 1871, daughter of Charles and Fanny Cummings of Laprairie. (page 47)

Cummings, Flora Ann
B-74, Flora Ann Cummings, baptized 6 May 1860, daughter of Charles and Sarah Cummings. (page 10)

Cummings, Francis Cuthbert Malcolm

B-439, Francis Cuthbert Malcolm Cummings, baptized 28 May 1876, son of Malcolm and Margaret Cummings. (page 55)

Cummings, Isabella

B-425, Isabella Cummings, baptized 25 April 1875, daughter of Charles and Fanny Cummings of Laprairie. (page 54)

Cummings, Isabelle

B-201, Isabelle Cummings, baptized 6 January 1864, daughter of Malcolm and Margaret Cummings, school master. (page 26)

Cummings, Isabelle

S-133, Isabella Cummings, of Portage la Prairie, age 1 year 8 months, buried 16 December 1877. (page 17)

Cummings, Jane

B-92, Jane Cummings, baptized 1 February 1861, daughter of Malcolm and Margaret Cummings. (page 12)

Cummings, Jeremiah George

S-40, Jeremiah George Cummings of Portage la Prairie, age 16 months, buried 12 August 1864. (page 5)

Cummings, Jerimiah George

B-163, Jeremiah George Cummings, baptized 9 March 1863, son of Charles and Sarah Cummings. (page 21)

Cummings, Margaret

B-132, Margaret Cummings, baptized 14 March 1862, daughter of an Indian woman. (page 17)

Cummings, Margaret

B-417, Margaret Cummings, baptized 20 September 1874, daughter of Malcolm and Margaret Cummings of Laprairie. (page 53)

Cummings, Mary Blanche

B-569, Mary Blanche Cummings, baptized 25 May 1883, daughter of Philip and Sarah Jane Cummings of Portage la Prairie. (page 72)

Cummings, Mary Christie
B-387, Mary Christie Cummings, baptized 16 June 1872, daughter of Malcom and Margaret Cummings of Laprairie. (page 49)

Cummings, Roderick George
B-440, Roderick George Cummings, baptized 18 June 1876, son of Charles and Fanny Cummings. (page 55)

Cummings, Sarah Gertrude
B-516, Sarah Gertrude Cummings, born 9 April 1881, baptized 19 June 1881, daughter of Charles and Fanny Cummings. (page 65)

Cummings, Walter John
B-475, Walter John Cummings, baptized 9 February 1879, son of Charles and Fanny Cummings (Sexton). (page 60)

Curtis, Cecilia
See William Gilbert and Cecilia Curtis

Curtis, Charles
S-102, Charles Curtis, of Portage la Prairie, age 59 days, buried 7 August 1874. (page 13)

Curtis, Charles W. Gavin
B-400, Charles W. Gavin Curtis, baptized 11 October 1873, son of Charles and Cecila Curtis of Laprairie. (page 50)

Curtis, Louise
B-351, Louise Curtis, baptized 16 October 1870, daughter of Charles and Cecilia Curtis. (page 44)

Curtis, Mary
See Joseph Buchanan and Mary Curtis

Cusitor, Ann
B-84, Ann Cusitor, baptized 30 September 1860, daughter of David and Margaret Cusitor. (page 11)

Cusitor, Annie
See Thomas James Smith and Annie Cusitor

Cusitor, David Magnus
B-536, David Magnus Cusitor, born 22 January 1882, son of David and Margaret Cusitor. (page 67)

Cusitor, David

S-188, David Cusitor, of Portage la Prairie, age 60 years and 7 months, buried 18 November 1882. (page 24)

Cusitor, Dinah Julia

B-476, Dinah Julia Cusitor, baptized 9 March 1879, daughter of David and Margaret Cusitor. (page 60)

Cusitor, Edith

B-511, Edith Cusitor, baptized 25 January 1880, daughter of David and Margaret Cusitor. (page 64)

Cusitor, Elizabeth Mary

B-304, Elizabeth Mary Cusitor, baptized 5 January 1868, daughter of David and Margaret Cusitor, St. Marys. (page 38)

Cusitor, George Alexander

B-460, George Alexander Cusitor, baptized 25 November 1877, son of David and Margaret Cusitor of Laprairie. (page 58)

Cusitor, James and Julia McKay

M-94, James Cusitor, age 28, of Portage la Prairie, son of David Cusitor, married 16 February 1881, Julia McKay, age 19, of Portage la Prairie, daughter of John Dougal McKay, by Henry George, Witnesses: Ann Cusitor and Joseph McKay. (page 48)

Cusitor, James

B-144, Jemima Cusitor, baptized 21 September 1862, daughter of David and Margaret Cusitor. (page 18)

Cusitor, Jane

B-258, Jane Cusitor, baptized 4 March 1866, daughter of David and Margaret Cusitor of Portage la Prairie. (page 33)

Cusitor, Jemima

See Edwin Spence and Jemima Cusitor

Cusitor John

B-566, John Cusitor (illegitimate), baptized 12 April 1883, son of John Cusitor and Matilda of Portage la Prairie. (page 71)

Cusitor, Louisa Florence

B-544, Louisa Florence Huddlestone, born 10 April 1882, baptized 11 June 1882, daughter of James [Cusitor] and Julie Huddlestone [McKay] of Portage la Prairie. (page 68)

Cusitor, Margaret Catherine

B-338, Margaret Catherine Cusitor, baptized 3 April 1870, daughter of David and Margaret Cusitor. (page 43)

Cusitor, Rosina

B-404, Rosina Cusitor, baptized 28 December 1873, daughter of David and Margaret Custor of Laprairie. (page 51)

Cusitor, Rosina Maria

B-431, Rosina Maria Cusitor, baptized 24 October 1875, daughter of David and Margaret Cusitor of Laprairie. (page 54)

Cusitor, Rosine

S-110, Rosine Cusitor, daughter of David Cusitor, of Portage la Prairie, age 17 months, buried April 1875. (page 14)

Cusitor, Sarah Harriet

B-385, Sarah Harriet Cusitor, baptized 12 May 1872, daughter of David and Margaret Cusitor of Laprairie. (page 49)

Cusitor, William

B-223, William Cusitor, baptized 22 May 1864, son of David and Margaret Cusitor of Portage la Prairie. (page 28)

Daniel, Allen John

B-316, Allen John Daniel, baptized 6 September 1868, son of John and Mary Daniel, Fort Pelly, HBC servant. (page 40)

Daniel, Elizabeth Catherine

B-344, Elizabeth Catherine Daniel, baptized 29 May 1870, daughter of John and Mary Daniel. Grandchild of Allen McIver. (page 43)

Daniel, John and Mary Margaret McIver

M-43, John Daniel, age 22, of Laprairie, son of William Daniel, married 5 July 1867, Mary Margaret McIver, age 18, of Laprairie, daughter of Allen McIver, by Henry George, Witnesses: Nancy Corrigal, George Garrioch, Mary Ga... (page 22)

Daniel, William

B-37, William Daniel, baptized 8 November 1857, son of William Daniel (Hudson Bay Company) and Indian Woman of Fort Ellice. (page 5)

Davis, Anthony

B-355, Anthony Davis, baptized 13 January 1871, son of George and Catherine Davis of Laprairie (HBC). (page 45)

Davis, Nellie

See Wellington Conniff and Nellie Davis

Davis, William Herbert

B-328, William Herbert Davis, baptized 16 May 1869, son of George and Catherine Davis, St. Marys. (page 41)

Denton, Sarah

B-547, Sarah Denton, born 26 February 1882, daughter of William Thomas and Rachel Denton of Portage la Prairie. (page 69)

Desjarlais, Margaret

See William Sutherland and Margaret Desjarlais

Desmarais, Absolom

B-59, Absolom Desmarais, baptized 5 September 1859, son of Absolom Larocque and Elise Desmarais. (page 8)

Desmarais, Amelia Harriet

B-292, Amelia Harriet Desmarais, baptized 23 July 1867, daughter of _?_ and Elizabeth, La Prairie. (page 37)

Desmarais, Baptiste and Margaret Tanner

M-69, Baptiste Desmarais, widower, of Westbourne, m. 11 Sep 1871, Margaret Tanner, (widow) of Westbourne, by Henry George, Witness: Catherine Anderson. (page 32)

Desmarais, Caroline

S-49, Caroline Desmarais, of Portage la Prairie, age 6 months, buried 13 November 1865. (page 7)

Desmarais, Catherine Margaret

See George Washington Hodgson and Catherine Margaret Desmarais

Desmarais, Catherine

S-173, Catherine Desmarais, of Portage la Prairie, age 22 years, buried 13 March 1881. (page 22)

Desmarais, Catherine

See Pierre Cadot and Catherine Desmarais

Desmarais, Charles and Mary Ann Whitford

M-45, Charles Desmarais, of St. Margarets, son of Baptiste Desmarais, married 12 September 1867, Mary Ann Whitford, of St. Marys, daughter of James Whitford, by Henry George, Witnesses: James Francis Sanderson and Isabelle Ann Inkster. (page 23)

Desmarais, Charles

B-142, Charles Desmarais, baptized 24 August 1862, son of Francis and Catherine Desmarais. (page 18)

Desmarais, Elizabeth

See Thomas Anderson and Elizabeth Desmarais

Desmarais, Flora Sarah

B-58, Flora Sarah Desmarais, baptized 7 September 1859, daughter of Baptiste and Sophia Desmarais. (page 8)

Desmarais, Frances

S-70, Francis Desmarais, of Portage la Prarie, age 30 years, buried 28 July 1868. (page 9)

Desmarais, Frances

See J. Finley Wray and Frances Desmarais

Desmarais, Francis and Catherine Pocha

M-5, Francis Desmarais, age 27, of Portage la Prairie, son of Charles Desmarais, married 23 December 1858, Catherine Pocha, age 30 (widow of an Indian) of Portage la Prairie, by William Cochran, Witnesses: Joseph Tate and Charles Desmarais. (page 3)

Desmarais, George Albert

S-61, George Albert Desmarais of Portage la Prairie, age 6 months, buried 18 September 1867. (page 8)

Desmarais, Harriet

B-371, Harriet Desmarais, baptized 26 July 1871, daughter of Michel and Isabella Desmarais of Westbourne. (page 47)

Desmarais, Henry Charles

B-280, Henry Charles Desmarais, baptized 21 November 1866, son of Betsy Desmarais of Laprairie. (page 35)

Desmarais, Henry Thomas

B-60, Henry Thomas Desmarais, baptized 5 September 1869. [entry crossed out] (page 8)

Desmarais, Isabelle

B-310, Isabelle Desmarais, baptized 18 May 1868, daughter of Mary of St. Marys. (page 39)

Desmarais, Isabelle

S-68, Isabelle Desmarais, of Portage la Prairie, age 8 weeks, buried 28 June 1868. (page 9)

Desmarais, Joseph

B-324, Joseph Desmarais, baptized 7 March 1869, son of Michel and Isabelle Desmarais, St. Marys. (page 41)

Desmarais, Joseph

S-48, Joseph Desmarais of Portage la Prairie, age 15 years, buried 4 November 1865. (page 6)

Desmarais, Margaret

B-369, Margaret Desmarais, baptized 26 July 1871, daughter of Charles and Mary Ann Desmarais of Westbourne. (page 47)

Desmarais, Mary Ann

See Samuel Smith and Mary Ann Desmarais

Desmarais, Mary

See John Favel and Mary Desmarais

Desmarais, Michel and Isabella Bird

M-38, Michel Desmarais, age 22, of St. Marys, son of Charles Desmarais, married 17 January 1866, Isabelle Bird, (widow), of St. Marys, daughter of William Sinclair, by Henry George, Witnesses: Robert Cook, Peter Henderson, James Sinclair. (page 19)

Desmarais, Patrick

B-269, Patrick Desmarais, baptized 28 June 1866, son of Eliza Desmarais of Portage la Prairie. (page 34)

Desmarais, Rebecca

B-31, Rebecca Desmarais, baptized 21 June 1857, daughter of Baptiste and Sophia Desmarais. (page 4)

Desmarais, Rosina

B-470, Rosina Desmarais, baptized 26 August 1878, daughter of Catherine Desmarais of Portage la Prairie. (page 59)

Desmarais, Thomas

B-143, Thomas Desmarais, baptized 7 September 1862, son of Francois and Catherine Desmarais. (page 18)

Desmarais, Victoria Harriet

B-128, Victoria Harriet Desmarais, baptized 2 February 1862, daughter of Baptiste and Sophia Desmarais of High Bluff. (page 16)

Desmarais, Victoria Harriet

B-44, Victoria Harriet Desmarais, baptized 31 October 1858, daughter of Charles and Harriet Desmarais. (page 6)

Desmarais, Victoria

S-50, Victoria Desmarais of Portage la Prairie, age 7 years, buried 26 January 1865. (page 7)

Desmarais, William Thomas

B-3, William Thomas Desmarais, baptized 9 December 1855, son of Baptiste and Sophie Desmarais of Portage la Prairie. (page 1)

Diehl, John and Grace Carrie

M-108, John Diehl, age 29, of Portage la Prairie, son of Jacob Diehl, married 17 October 1883, Grace Carrie, age 28, of Portage la Prairie, daughter of William Carrie, by A. C. Fortin. (page 55)

Dobson, Robert and Rose Coloqhson

M-107, Robert Dobson, age 32, son of Robert Dobson, married 21 June 1883, Rose Coloqhson, age 26, of Portage la Prairie, daughter of Coloquhson, by A. C. Fortin. (page 54)

Donald, Elizabeth

See David Favel and Elizabeth Donald

Donald, Mary

B-296, Mary Donald, baptized 12 September 1867, daughter of _?_ and Elizabeth. (page 37)

Donald, Sarah Jane

B-346, Sarah Jane Donald, baptized 5 June 1870, daughter of Elizabeth Donald.

Donely, Jane

See Edwin Edward Newall and Jane Donely

Donley, Eliza

See Gardner Stevens Greenlay and Eliza Donley

Drain, David

B-554, David Drain, born 10 August 1882, son of David and Flora Drain of Portage la Prairie. (page 554)

Drever, James

B-25, James Drever, baptized 3 September 1865, son of James and Margaret Drever Trader at G. Sask. River. (page 32)

Drever, Jemima

B-176, Jemima Drever, baptized 28 June 1863, daughter of James and Margaret Drever. (page 22)

Ellis, George

S-116, George Ellis, of Portage la Prairie, age 39 years, buried 3 December 1876. (page 15)

Enor [?], J. Baptiste

S-64, J. Batpiste Enor [?], of H. B. Co. Fort, age 56, buried 12 March 1868. (page 8)

Erasmus, Mary Ann

See Andrew Peterson and Mary Ann Erasmus

Favel, Alexander

B-444, Alexander Favel, baptized 21 September 1876, son of William and Ann Favel of Laprairie. (page 56)

Favel, Alexander

S-123, Alexander Favel, of Portage la Prairie, age 8 months, buried 31 March 1877. (page 16)

Favel, Charles

B-359, Charles Favel, baptized 19 March 1871, son of William and Ann Favel of Laprairie. (page 45)

Favel, Charles

B-422, Charles Favel, baptized 6 December 1874, son of Charles and Ann Favel of Laprairie. (page 53)

Favel, David and Elizabeth Donald

M-71, David Favel, age 19, of St. Marys, son of Richard Favel, married 31 January 1872, Elizabeth Donald, age 21, of St. Marys, by Henry George, Witness: Richard Favel. (page 33)

Favel, David

B-563, David Favel, baptized 22 March 1883, son of David and Elizabeth Favel of Portage la Prairie. (page 71)

Favel, David James

B-340, David James Favel, baptized 6 April 1870, son of Samuel Favel and Heathen. (page 43)

Favel, David

S-192, David Favel, of Portage la Prairie, age 10 days, buried 25 March 1883. (page 24)

Favel, Edwin

B-496, Edwin Favel, baptized 12 April 1880, son of David and Elizabeth Favel. (page 62)

Favel, Elizabeth

B-428, Elizabeth Favel, baptized 30 May 1875, daughter of David and Elizabeth Favel of Laprairie. (page 54)

Favel, Elizabeth Harriet

B-82, Elizabeth Harriet Favel, baptized 16 September 1860, daughter of Richard and Euphemia Favel. (page 11)

Favel, Euphemia

S-175, Euphemia Favel, of Portage la Prairie, age 66 years, buried 5 May 1881. (page 22)

Favel, Henry

B-463, Henry Favel, baptized 3 February 1878, son of David and Elizabeth Favel of Portage la Prairie. (page 58)

Favel, Henry George

B-295, Henry George Favel, baptized 16 August 1867, son of Samuel Favel and Heathen woman, La Prairie. (page 37)

Favel, Henry George
S-90, Henry George Favel, of Portage la Prairie, age 6 years, buried 3 January 1873. (page 12)

Favel, John and Mary Desmarais
M-52, John Favel, age 27, widower, of Long Lake, son of John Favel, married 20 September 1869, Mary Desmarais, age 26, of St. Marys, daughter of Charles Desmarais, by Henry George, Witnesses: John Corrigal and Mathilde Hodgson. (page 27)

Favel, John James
B-268, John James Favel, baptized 25 June 1866, son of Mary Favel of Portage la Prairie. (page 34)

Favel, John James
S-65, John James Favel, of La Prairie, age 1 year and 8 months, buried 17 March 1868. (page 9)

Favel, Joseph
S-51, Joseph Favel son of Mary, of Portage la Prairie, age 18 months, buried 5 February 1865. (page 7)

Favel, Joseph Samuel
S-108, Joseph Samuel Favel, son of Samuel Favel, of Portage la Prairie, age 6 months, buried 13 April 1875. (page 14)

Favel, Margaret Ann
B-393, Margaret Ann Favel, baptized 19 January 1873, daughter of David and Elizabeth Favel of Laprairie. (page 50)

Favel, Margaret
See David Simpson and Margaret Favel

Favel, Mary Ann
B-309, Mary Ann Favel, baptized 30 April 1868, daughter of Mary, St. Marys. (page 39)

Favel, Mary Ann
B-408, Mary Ann Favel, baptized 29 March 1874, daughter of William and Ann Favel. (page 51)

Favel, Mary
S-109, Mary Favel, daughter of Richard Favel, of Porage la Prairie, age __, buried 23 April 1875. (page 14)

Favel, Richard

S-92, Richard Favel, of Portage la Prairie, age 60 years, buried 30 April 1873. (page 12)

Favel, Samuel

S-111, Samuel Favel, son of Richard Favel, of Portage la Prairie, age 40 years, buried 8 July 1875. (page 14)

Favel, Sarah

B-20, Sarah Favel, baptized 17 August 1856, daughter of Richard and Euphemia Favel of Portage la Prairie. (page 3)

Favel, Sarah

See Samuel Geddings and Sarah Favel

Favel, Victoria

B-152, Victoria Favel, baptized 30 November 1862, daughter of Richard and Euphemia Favel of High Bluff. (page 19)

Favel, William and Ann Gaddy

M-36, William Favel, age 21, of St. Marys, son of Richard Favel, married 14 December 1865, Ann Gaddy, age 18, of St. Marys, by Henry George, Witness: Peter Henderson. (page 18)

Favel, William Peter

B-282, William Peter Favel, baptized 3 February 1867, son of William and Ann Favel, of LaPrairie. (page 36)

Field, Edward and Catherine McIver

M-61, Edward Field, age 24, Hudson Bay Company Clerk, of St. Marys, son of Samuel Field, married 10 May 1871, Catherine McIver, age 18, of St. Marys, daughter of Allen McIver, by Henry George, Witness: John Gordon. (page 31)

Field, Helen L.

B-405, Helen L. Field, baptized 15 March 1874, daughter of Francis and Rhoda Jane Field of Laprairie. (page 51)

Field, Milton

B-432, Milton Field, baptized 31 October 1875, son of Francis and Roda Jane Field of Laprairie. (page 54)

Flynn, Eva Maude

B-Eva Maude Flynn, born 20 April 1881, baptized 10 May 1881, daughter of John and Ellen Flynn. (page 65)

Forbister, John
B-240, John Forbister, baptized 23 April 1865, son of James and Catherine Forbister of Long Lake. (page 30)

Fortin, Daisy Geraldine
B-552, Daisy Geraldine Fortin, born 12 October 1882, daughter of Alfred Louis and Louise Fortin. (page 69)

Foulds, Henry
B-388, Henry Foulds, baptized 16 June 1872, son of John and Nancy Foulds of High Bluff. (page 49)

Fowler, Flora Ann
B-298, Flora Ann Fowler, baptized 27 November 1867, daughter of John and Ann Fowler, St. Margarets P.L.P. (page 38)

Franks, Alfred
B-91, Alfred Franks, baptized 20 January 1861, son of James and Sarah Franks. (page 12)

Franks, King Israel
B-166, King Israel Franks, baptized 29 March 1863, son of James and Sarah Franks. (page 21)

Gaddy, Alexander James
B-260, Alexander James Gaddy, baptized 29 April 1866, son of Alexander and Margaret Gaddy of Portage la Prairie. (page 260)

Gaddy, Ann
B-254, Ann Gaddy, baptized 28 November 1865 daughter of a Heathen Indian of Portage la Prairie. (page 32)

Gaddy, Ann
See William Favel and Ann Gaddy

Gaddy, Barbara Ellen
B-315, Barbara Ellen Gaddy, baptized 21 June 1868, daughter of Alex and Margaret Gaddy, St. Marys. (page 40)

Gaddy, Jane
B-186, Jane Gaddy, baptized 6 October 1863, daughter of Alexander and Margaret Gaddy. (page 24)

Gaddy, William

B-117, William Gaddy, baptized 27 October 1862, son of Alexander and Margaret Gaddy. (page 15)

Garden, Emma Margaret

B-567, Emma Garden, baptized 5 April 1883, daughter of George and Catherine Garden of Portage la Prairie. (page 71)

Garden, George F. S. and Catherine Bird

M-83, George F. S. Garden, age 29, of Portage la Prairie, married 9 January 1878, Catherine Bird, age 19, of Portage la Prairie, daughter of Frederick Bird, by Henry George, Witnesses: John James Setter and Flora Cummings. (page 42)

Garner, George Wellington

S-186, George Wellington Garner, of Portage la Prairie, age 8 months, buried 6 September 1882. (page 24)

Garrioch, Adelaide Ann

B-394, Adelaide Ann Garrioch, baptized 2 February 1873, daughter of William and Mary Garrioch of Laprairie. (page 50)

Garrioch, Albert Clarence

B-291, Albert Clarence Garrioch, baptized 21 July 1867, son of William and Mary Garrioch, La Prairie. (page 37)

Garrioch, Alice Edith

B-325, Alice Edith Garrioch, baptized 11 April 1869, daughter of William and Mary Garrioch, St. Marys. (page 41)

Garrioch, Andrew George

B-349, Andrew George Garrioch, baptized 25 September 1870, son of Gavin and Hannah Garrioch of Portage la Prairie. (page 44)

Garrioch, Charles Palmer

B-398, Charles Palmer Garrioch, baptized 8 June 1873, son of Gavin and Hannah Garrioch of Laprairie. (page 50)

Garrioch, Dinah

B-251, Dinah Garrioch, baptized 29 October 1865, daughter of William and Mary Garrioch of Portage la Prairie. (page 32)

Garrioch, Elizabeth
> See Patrick Bruce and Elizabeth Garrioch

Garrioch, Ella L.
> B-464, Ella L. Garrioch, baptized 17 February 1878, daughter of George and George Anne Garrioch. (page 58)

Garrioch, Ellen
> B-38, Ellen Garrioch, baptized 10 January 1858, daughter of John and Eliza Garrioch. (page 5)

Garrioch, Ellen
> See Edward Pelly and Ellen Garrioch

Garrioch, Emma Catherine
> B-357, Emma Catherine Garrioch, baptized 12 March 1871, daughter of William and Mary Garrioch of Laprairie. (page 45)

Garrioch, Emmeline
> B-66, Emmeline Garrioch, baptized 11 December 1859, daughter of Peter and Margaret Garrioch. (page 9)

Garrioch, Flora
> B-5, Flora Garrioch, baptized 10 February 1856, daughter of John and Eliza Garrioch of Portage la Prairie. (page 1)

Garrioch, Flora
> See Andrew Maxwell and Flora Garrioch

Garrioch, Florence Jane
> B-583, Florence Jane Garrioch baptized 19 October 1883, daughter of William H. and Jane Garrioch. (page 73)

Garrioch, George and Georgina Albright
> M-81, George Garrioch, of Portage la Prairie, son of John Garrioch, married 25 September 1876, Georgina Albright, age 18, of Portage la Prairie, by Henry George, Witnesses: John James Setter and Charles Cummings. (page 41)

Garrioch, George Anna
> S-181, George Anna Garrioch, of Portage la Prairie, age 24 years, buried 6 March 1882. (page 23)

Garrioch, George Hannah

B-540, George Hannah Garrioch, born 17 July 1881, baptized 1 April 1882, child of George and George Hannah Garrioch. (page 68)

Garrioch, Gilbert

B-53, Gilbert Garrioch, baptized 4 July 1859, son of William and Mary Garrioch. (page 7)

Garrioch, Gilbert Heber

S-80, Gilbert Heber Garrioch, of Portage la Prairie, age 13 years, buried _, June 1871. (page 10)

Garrioch, Harriet Jane

B-131, Harriet Jane Garrioch, baptized 9 March 1862, daughter of William and Mary Garrioch. (page 17)

Garrioch, Heber Charles

B-413, Heber Charles Garrioch, baptized 28 June 1874, son of William and Mary Garrioch of Laprairie. (page 52)

Garrioch, Henry

B-1, Henry Garrioch, baptized 30 September 1855, son of William and Mary Garrioch of Portage la Prairie. (page 1)

Garrioch, Henry

S-1, Henry Garrioch of Portage la Prairie, age 12 days, buried 3 October 1855. (page 1)

Garrioch, Henry Small

B-231, Henry Small Garrioch, baptized 18 December 1864, son of Gavin and Hannah Garrioch of Laprairie. (page 29)

Garrioch, James Hamilton

B-451, James Hamilton Garrioch, baptized 29 April 1877, son of William Hamilton and Jane Garrioch of Portage la Prairie. (page 57)

Garrioch, James Heber

S-6, James Heber Garrioch, of Portage la Prairie, age 4 years, buried 12 September 1857. (page 1)

Garrioch, Jemima

B-27, Jemima Garrioch, baptized 17 May 1857, daughter of William and Mary Garrioch. (page 4)

Garrioch, Jessy

B-81, Jessy Garrioch, baptized 16 September 1860, daughter of John and Eliza Garrioch. (page 11)

Garrioch, John

B-35, John Garrioch, baptized 20 September 1857, son of Peter and Margaret Garrioch. (page 5)

Garrioch, Luther Kelly

B-193, Luther Kelly Garrioch, baptized 21 November 1863, son of Gavin and Hannah Garrioch. (page 25)

Garrioch, Luther Kelly

S-26, Luther Kelly Garrioch, of Portage la Prairie, age 9 months, buried 6 January 1864. (page 4)

Garrioch, Margaret

B-191, Margaret Garrioch, baptized 31 October 1863, daughter of William and Mary Garrioch. (page 24)

Garrioch, Margaret Isabelle

B-238, Margaret Isabelle Garrioch, baptized 26 February 1865, daughter of Peter and Margaret Garrioch of Laprairie. (page 30)

Garrioch, Maria

B-256, Maria Garrioch, baptized 17 December 1865, daughter of John and Eliza Garrioch of Portage la Prairie. (page 32)

Garrioch, Mary Harriet

See John McVicar and Mary Harriet Garrioch

Garrioch, Mary Marian

B-86, Mary Marian Garrioch, baptized 21 October 1860, daughter of William and Mary Garrioch. (page 11)

Garrioch, Nancy

S-114, Nancy Garrioch, widow of William Garrioch, of Portage la Prairie, age 100 years, buried 15 November 1875. (page 15)

Garrioch, Richard

B-483, Richard Garrioch, baptized 15 Jun 1879, son of William and Henriette + Jane Garrioch of Portage la Prairie. (page 61)

Garrioch, Silas Jonas

S-34, Silas Jonas Garrioch, of Portage la Prairie, age 1 year, 6 months, buried 18 March 1864. (page 5)

Garrioch, Silas Jones

B-145, Silas Jones Garrioch, baptized 26 October 1862, son of Peter and Margaret Garrioch. (page 19)

Garrioch, Walter Pelly

B-99, Walter Pelly Garrioch, baptized 12 May 1861, son of Gavin and Hannah Garrioch. (page 13)

Garrioch, Walter Pelly

S-45, Walter Pelly Garrioch, of Portage la Prairie, age 3 years and 9 months, buried 13 January 1865. (page 6)

Garrioch, Walter Scott

B-189, Walter Scott Garrioch, baptized 17 October 1863, son of John and Eliza Garrioch. (page 24)

Garrioch, William Alexander

B-519, William Alexander Garrioch born 29 April 1881, son of William H. and Jane Garrioch. (page 65)

Garrioch, William C. Ridley

B-300, William C. Ridley Garrioch, baptized 2 December 1867, son of Peter and Margaret Garrioch, Westbourne, Catechist. (page 38)

Garrioch, William Hamilton and Jane White Wendle

M-77, William Hamilton Garrioch, age 23, of Portage la Prairie, son of Gavin Garrioch, married 18 August 1875, Jane White Wendle, age 18, daughter of James Wendle. (page 39)

Garrioch, William

S-22, William Garrioch of Portage la Prairie, age 18 years and 10 months, buried 6 May 1863. (page 3)

Garrioch, Winnifred Olivine Margaret

B-345, Winnifred Olivine Margaret Garrioch, baptized 5 June 1870, daughter of John and Eliza Garrioch. (page 44)

Geddings, Joseph Thomas

B-363, Joseph Thomas Geddings, baptized 9 June 1871, son of Samuel and Sarah Geddings of Laprairie. (page 46)

Geddings, Samuel and Sarah Favel

M-52, Samuel Geddings, age 18, of St. Marys, son of Benjamin Geddings, married 29 June 1870, Sarah Favel, age 15, of St. Marys, daughter of Richard Favel, by Henry George, Witnesses: Elizabeth Hodgson and James Henderson. (page 28)

Gee, Thomas Edward

B-553, Thomas Edward Gee, born 14 October 1882, son of John Edward and Jane Gee of Portage la Prairie. (page 70)

Gelly, Frederick Dawson

S-154, Frederick Dawson Gelly, of Simcoe, Ontario, age 49 years, buried 25 March 1880. (page 20)

George, Constance Jane

B-327, Constance Jane George, baptized 2 May 1869, daughter of Henry and Mary Anne George, St. Marys. (page 41)

George, Elizabeth Ann

See Walter M. Pratt and Elizabeth Ann George

George, Henry

S-178, Henry George, of Portage la Prairie, age 48 years, buried 9 August 1881. (page 23)

George, James Edward and Mary J. Parker

M-97, James Edward George, age 20, of Portage la Prairie, son of Henry George, married 3 May 1881, Mary J. Parker, age 20, of Portage la Prairie, daughter of John Parkier, by Henry George, Witness: John J. Setter. (page 49)

George, James Edward

B-100, James Edward George, baptized 27 May 1861, son of Henry and Mary Ann George (Weslyan). (page 13)

George, Jemima Maria

B-245, Jemima Maria George, baptized 18 June 1865, daughter of Henry and Mary Ann George missionary of Westbourne. (page 31)

George, Mary Emma

B-273, Mary Emma George, baptized 12 August 1866, daughter of Henry and Mary Ann George of Portage la Prairie. (page 35)

George, Peter and Ida Mowat

M-92, Peter George, age 32, of Portage la Prairie, son of Theodore George, married 15 December 1880, Ida Mowat, age 27, of Portage la Prairie, daughter of John Mowat, by Henry George. (page 47)

George, Sidney Edward

B-539, Sidney Edward George, baptized 30 March 1882, son of Edward and Minnie George of Portage la Prairie. (page 68)

George, Stewart Charles

B-549, Stewart Charles George, born May 2, 1882, baptisted 21 July 1882. [This entry is crossed out.] (page 69)

George, William Henry

B-52, William Henry George, baptized 19 June 1859, son of Henry and Mary Anne George, missionary. (page 7)

Gibault, Julia

See James Johnston and Julia Gibault

Gibeau, Mary

See James Park and Mary Gibeau

Gilbert, Emes

B-492, Emes Gilbert, baptized 18 January 1880, son of William and Cecile Gilbert. (page 62)

Gilbert, William and Cecilia Curtis

M-88, William Gilbert, age 34, of Portage la Prairie, married 14 October 1878, Ceclia Curtis, age 36, of Portage la Prairie, by Henry George. (page 45)

Giles, Annie

See John Blair and Annie Giles

Gill, Eliza

See Andrew Whitford and Eliza Gill

Gill, Harriet

See Robert Inkster and Harriet Gill

Gill, Sarah
See Thomas Sandison and Sarah Gill

Glenn, Ellen
S-72, Ellen Glenn, of Portage la Prairie, age 73 eyars, buried 19 October 1868. (page 9)

Glenn, Joseph and Martha Armstrong
M-103, Joseph Glenn, age 33, of Gladstone, son of Samuel Glenn and Esther, married 15 February 1883, Martha Armstrong, age 34, of Portage Plains, daughter of John Armstrong and Maria, by A. C. Fortin. (page 52)

Goldie, Catherine Eliza
B-555, Catherine Eliza Goldie, baptized 10 December 1882, daughter of A. B. D. and Elizabeth Grace Goldie of Portage la Prairie, a Brewer. (page 70)

Gordon, Erma Margaret
S-191, Erma Margaret Gordon, of Portage la Prairie, age 1 day, buried 5 April 1883. (page 24)

Gowan, Frances
S-151, Frances Gowan, of Portage Creek, age 6 months, buried 2 April 1879. (page 19)

Gowan, Mary Ann
S-149, Mary Ann Gowan, of Portage Creek, age 69, buried 2 September 1879. (page 19)

Gowan, William
S-150, William Gowan, of Portage Creek, age 18 years, buried 15 September 1879. (page 19)

Green, Jesse
S-107, Jessie Green, of Portage la Prairie, age 65, buried 9 April 1875. (page 14)

Greenlay, Gardner Stevens and Eliza Donley
M-71, Gardner Stevens Grelay, age 26, of St. Marys, son of L. Greenlay, married 25 April 1873, Eliza Donley, age 16, of St. Marys, daughter of Wm. Donley, by Henry George, Witnesses: Alexander McLean, Jane Donley, Ann Donley. (page 36)

Grusbach Arthur and Emma Maria Hodgins
M-82, Arthur Grusbach, age 37, widower of Swan River, son of William Robert Grusbach, married 26 March 1877, Emma Maria Hodgins, age 26, of Winnipeg, daughter of Samuel Hodgins, by Henry George, Witnesses: William Lyons and Jim Lyons. (page 41)

Halcrow, Ann Maria

See Peter Henderson and Ann Maria Halcrow

Halcrow, Annabelle

S-133, Annabelle Halcrow, of Portage la Prairie, age 1 year 4 months, buried 7 August 1877. (page 16)

Halcrow, Catherine

B-162, Catherine Halcrow, baptized 23 February 1863, daughter of David and Elizabeth Halcrow. (page 21)

Halcrow, Catherine

S-83, Catherine Halcrow, of Portage la Prairie, age 8 years, buried 22 September 1871. (page 11)

Halcrow, Elizabeth

B-290, Elizabeth Halcrow, baptized 30 June 1867, daughter of David and Elizabeth Halcrow, La Prairie. (page 37)

Halcrow, Elizabeth

S-99, Elizabeth Halcrow, daughter of David Halcrow of La Prairie, age 7 years, buried 6 March 1874. (page 13)

Halcrow, Euphemia

B-378, Euphemia Halcrow, baptized 31 March 1872, daughter of David Halcrow and Elizabeth, of Laprairie. (page 48)

Halcrow, Hannah Bella

B-437, Hannah Bella Halcrow, baptized 27 March 1876, daughter of Letita Halcrow of Laprairie. (page 55)

Halcrow, Hannah

See John Michel Anderson and Hannah Halcrow

Halcrow, Joseph

B-243, Joseph Halcrow, baptized 29 May 1865, son of David and Elizabeth Halcrow of Laprairie. (page 31)

Halcrow, Mary

See John Henry Anderson and Mary Halcrow

Halcrow, Roderick James

B-471, Roderick James Halcrow, baptized 26 August 1878, son of Ann Halcrow of Portage la Prairie. (page 59)

Halcrow, Roderick James

S-144, Roderick James Halcrow, of Portage la Prairie, age 10 months 10 days, buried 9 December 1878. (page 18)

Halcrow, Sophia

B-333, Sophia Halcrow, baptized 14 November 1869, daughter of David and Elizabeth Halcrow. (page 42)

Hallett, Alexander

B-227, Alexander Hallett, baptized 5 June 1864, son of Henry and Ellen Hallett of Poplar Point. (page 29)

Hallett, Ann

See Charles Bird and Ann Hallett

Hallett, Charles

B-126, Charles Hallett, baptized 19 January 1862, son of Henry Hallett. (page 16)

Harmponth, Sarah

S-28, Sarah Harmponth, of Poplar Point, age 4 years, buried 10 January 1864. (page 4)

Hay, Mary

S-101, Mary Hay, daughter of Charles Hay, of Portage la Prairie, age 3 days, buried 7 March 1874. (page 13)

Hellyer, Charles

S-79, Charles Hellyer, of Portage la Prairie, age 60 years, buried 7 May 1871. (page 10)

Henderson, Agnes Ann

B-533, Agnes Ann Henderson, born 18 August 1881, daughter of Eliza Henderson. (page 67)

Henderson, Agnes

B-473, Agnes Henderson, baptized 10 November 1878, daughter of James and Mary Henderson of Laprairie. (page 60)

Henderson, Albert

B-493, Albert Henderson, baptized 15 February 1880, son of Charles and Barbara Henderson. (page 62)

Henderson, Alexander Charles

B-423, Alexander Charles Henderson, baptized 24 January 1874, son of James and Mary Henderson of Laprairie. (page 53)

Henderson, Ann

B-537, Ann Henderson, baptized 19 January 1882, daughter of Charles and Barbara Henderson of Portage la Prairie. (page 68)

Henderson, Annabella

B-448, Anabella Henderson, baptized 26 November 1876, daughter of James and Mary Henderson of Laprairie. (page 56)

Henderson, Charlotte

S-100, Charlotte Henderson, of Portage la Prairie, age 90 years, buried 5 January 1874. (page 13)

Henderson, Edward

B-458, Edward Henderson, baptized 9 September 1877, son of Charles and Barbara Henderson of Portage la Prairie. (page 58)

Henderson, Eliza

B-322, Eliza Henderson, baptized 7 November 1869, daughter of Peter and Ann Henderson. (page 42)

Henderson, Elizabeth

B-430, Elizabeth Henderson, baptized 3 October 1874, daughter of Peter and Ann Henderson of Laprairie. (page 54)

Henderson, Ellen

B-311, Ellen Henderson, baptized 9 May 1868, daughter of Peter and Ann Henderson, St. Marys. (page 39)

Henderson, George

B-581, George Henderson, baptized 16 September 1883, son of Peter and Ann Henderson. (page 73)

Henderson, Hannah

B-365, Hannah Henderson, baptized 13 August 1871, daughter of Peter and Ann Henderson of Laprairie. (page 46)

Henderson, Henry Charles

S-162, Henry Charles Henderson, of Portage la Prairie, age 6 months, buried 19 July 1880. (page 21)

Henderson, Henry George

B-255, Henry George Henderson, baptized 10 December 1865, son of Peter and Ellen Henderson of Portage la Prairie. (page 32)

Henderson, Margaret Maria

B-331, Margaret Maria Henderson, baptized 3 November 1869, daughter of [Peter and Anna Maria Henderson]. (page 42)

Henderson, Maria

B-462, Maria Henderson, baptized 30 December 1877, daughter of Peter and Ann Henderson of Portage la Prairie. (page 58)

Henderson, Maria

See Alexander Sanderson and Maria Henderson

Henderson, Mary Ann

B-401, Mary Ann Henderson, baptized 26 October 1873, daughter of Peter and Ann Marie Henderson of Laprairie. (page 51)

Henderson, Mary Helen

B-565, Mary Helen Henderson, baptized 12 April 1883, daughter of William and Prisilla Henderson of Portage la Prairie. (page 71)

Henderson, Mary Helen

B-565, Mary Helen Henderson, baptized 12 April 1883, daughter of William and Prisilla Henderson of Portage la Prairie. (page 71)

Henderson, Mary Matilda

B-175, Mary Mathida Henderson, baptized 21 June 1863, daughter of Peter and Ellen Henderson. (page 22)

Henderson, Peter and Ann Maria Halcrow

M-40, Peter Henderson, age 20, of St. Marys, son of Peter Henderson, married 21 February 1867, Ann Maria Halcrow, age 18, of St. Marys, daughter of David Halcrow, by Henry George. (page 20)

Herbert, John

B-518, John Herbert, born 16 July 1881, son of James and Ellen Hubert. (page 65)

Herbert, John

S-177, John Herbert, of Portage la Prairie, age 2 years, buried 9 August 1881. (page 23)

Higginson, Florence

B-457, Florence Higginson, baptized 2 September 1877, daughter of Samuel Charles and Mary Higginson of Portage la Prairie. (page 58)

Higginson, Harriet

B-438, Harriet Higginson, baptized 17 May 1876, daughter of Samuel and Mary Higginson of Laprairie. (page 55)

Higginson, Samuel Charles and Mary Byers

M-75, Samuel Charles Higginson, age 24, of Portage la Prairie, son of George Higginson, married 28 September 1874, Mary Byers, age 18, of Portage la Prairie, daughter of Richard Byers, by Henry George, Witnesses: Richard Byers and William Byers. (page 38)

Hillyer, Charles

B-14, Charles Hillyer, baptized 15 June 1856, son of an Indian of Portage la Prairie. (page 2)

Hillyer, James

B-18, James Hillyer, baptized 15 June 1856, son of Charles and Maria Hillyer. (page 3)

Hillyer, Maria

B-15, Maria Hillyer, baptized 15 June 1856, wife of Charles Hillyer. (page 2)

Hillyer, Peter

B-16, Peter Hillyer, baptized 15 June 1856, son of Charles and Maria Hillyer. (page 2)

Hillyer, William

B-17, William Hillyer, baptized 15 June 1856, son of Charles and Maria Hillyer. (page 3)

Hodges, Fanny

B-368, Fanny Hodges, baptized 26 July 1871, daughter of George and Catherine Margaret Hodges of Laprairie. (page 46)

Hodges, William Rupert

B-182, William Rupert Hodges, baptized 23 August 1863, son of George and Catherine Margaret Hodges of High Bluff. (page 23)

Hodgins, Emma Maria

See Arthur Grusbach and Emma Maria Hogdins

Hodgson, Adelaide Harriet

B-277, Adelaide Harriet Hodgson, baptized 28 October 1866, daughter of William and Nancy Hodgson of Laprairie. (page 35)

Hodgson, Ann Elizabeth

See Thomas Corrigal and Ann Elizabeth Hodgson

Hodgson, Charlotte

S-131, Charlotte Hodgson, of St.Andrews, age 70, buried 5 July 1877. (page 16)

Hodgson, Edward

B-335, Edward Hodgson, baptized 27 February 1870, son of William and Nancy Hodgson. (page 42)

Hodgson, Emma Margaret

B-224, Emma Margaret Hodgson, baptized 29 May 1864, daughter of William and Ann Hodgson of Portage la Prairie. (page 28)

Hodgson, Emma

S-41, Emma Hodgson of Portage la Prairie, age 4 months, buried 12 September 1864. (page 6)

Hodgson, George Washington and Catherine Margaret Desmarais

M-22, George Washington Hodges, age _, of Poplar Bluff, married 27 November 1862, Catherine Margaret Desmarais, age _, daughter of Baptiste Desmarais, by William Cochran, Witnesses: William Clark and J. Finlay Wray. (page 11)

Hodgson, Isabelle

B-253, Isabella Hodgson, baptized 23 October 1865, daughter of William and Nancy Hodgson of Portage la Prairie. (page 253)

Hodgson, Isabelle

S-46, Isabelle Hodgson, of Portage la Prairie, age 2 weeks, buried 24 October 1865. (page 6)

Hodgson, John

B-198, John Hodgson, baptized 6 December 1863, son of Catherine Hodgson. (page 25)

Hodgson, John

S-106, John Hodgson, of High Bluff, age 80 years, buried 10 January 1875. (page 14)

Hodgson, John

S-43, John Hodgson, of Portage la Prairie, age 60 years, buried 3 December 1864. (page 6)

Hodgson, Lydia Jane

B-386, Lydia Jane Hodgson, baptized 9 June 1872, daughter of Wm. and Nancy Hodgson. (page 49)

Hodgson, Mary

B-219, Mary Hodgson, baptized 13 March 1864, adult Indian of Portage la Prairie. (page 28)

Hodgson, Mary

S-23, Mary Hodgson, of Portage la Prairie, age 30 years, buried 4 August 1863. (page 3)

Hodgson, Matilda

See Joseph Pocha and Matilda Hodgson

Hodgson, Sarah

B-218, Sarah Hodgson (adopted), baptized 13 March 1864, daughter of John and __ Hodgson of Portage la Prairie. (page 28)

Hodgson, Thomas

S-10, Thomas Hodgson, of Portage la Prairie, age 2 months, buried 22 April 1858. (page 2)

Hodson, Albert

B-105, Albert Hodson, baptized 21 July 1861, son of William and Ann Hodson, carpenter and miller. (page 14)

Hodson, Catherine

B-11, Catherine Hodson, baptized 15 June 1856, wife of William Hodson (Indian). (page 2)

Hodson, John

B-12, John Hodson, baptized 15 June 1856, son of William and Catherine Hodson (Indian) (page 2)

Hodson, Joseph

B-54, Joseph Hodson, baptized 17 July 1859, son of William and Ann Hodson. (page 7)

Hodson, Margaret

B-13, Margaret Hodson, baptized 15 June 1856, daughter of William and Catherine Hodson (Indian) (page 2)

Hodson, Mary

B-70, Mary Hodson (adult), baptized 5 March 1860, daughter of William and Maria (Indians). (page 9)

Hodson, Thomas

B-39, Thomas Hodson, baptized 14 March 1858, son of William and Ann Hodson. (page 5)

Hodson, William

B-10, William Hodson, baptized 15 June 1856, An Indian of LaPrairie, Paheahtawan). (page 2)

Horsfall, Eliza

S-69, Eliza Horsfall, of Portage la Prairie, age 16 years, buried 6 July 1868. (page 9)

Hourie, Elizabeth Jane

B-297, Elizabeth Jane Hourie, baptized 13 October 1867, daughter of Thomas and Agnes Hourie, St. Andrews. (page 38)

Howard, Louis Meredith

B-455, Louis Meredith Howard, baptized 12 July 1877, son of Rice and Lavina Howard of Portage la Prairie. (page 57)

Howse, Andrew

B-109, Andrew Howse, baptized 1 September 1861, son of Joseph and Elizabeth Howse. (page 14)

Howse, Anne Margaret

B-22, Anne Margaret Howse, baptized 5 October 1856, daughter of Henry and Elizabeth Howse. (page 3)

Howse, Charlotte

B-169, Charlotte Howse, baptized 20 April 1863, daughter of Henry and Elizabeth Mary Howse. (page 22)

Howse, Charlotte

S-32, Charlotte Howse of Portage la Prairie, age 10 months, buried 16 February 1864. (page 4)

Howse, Jane

B-43, Jane Howse, baptized 9 September 1858, daughter of Joseph and Elizabeth Howse. (page 6)

Howse, Jane

B-46, Jane Howse, baptized 24 January 1859, daughter of Henry and Elizabeth Howse. (page 6)

Howse, John

B-34, John Howse, baptized 13 September 1857, son of Henry and Elizabeth Howse. (page 5)

Howse, Joseph and Elizabeth Anderson

M-3, Joseph Howse of Portage la Prairie, son of Henry Howse, married 21 January 1858, Elizabeth Anderson of Portage la Prairie, daughter of Thomas Anderson, by William Cochran. (page 2)

Howse, Joseph

B-2, Joseph Howse, baptized 2 December 1855, son of Henry and Elizabeth Howse of Portage la Prairie. (page 1)

Howse, Maria

B-209, Maria Howse, baptized 21 February 1864, daughter of Joseph and Elizabeth Howse of Portage la Prairie. (page 27)

Howse, Mary

B-21, Mary Howse of Portage la Prairie, age 1-1/2 years, buried 19 September 1862. (page 3)

Howse, Mary

B-96, Mary Howse, baptized 31 March 1861, son of Henry and Elizabeth Howse. (page 12)

Howse, Matilda

B-236, Matilda Howse, baptized 15 January 1865, daughter of Henry and Elizabeth Howse of Laprairie. (page 30)

Howse, Thomas Henry

B-65, Thomas Henry Howse, baptized 3 December 1859, son of Joseph and Elizabeth Howse. (page 9)

Huddleston, Alexander M.

B-266, Alexander M. Huddleston, baptized 24 June 1866, son of Thomas and Margaret Huddleston of Laprairie. (page 34)

Huddleston, Elizabeth Victoria

B-265, Elizabeth Victoria Huddleston, baptized 24 June 1866, daughter of Thomas and Margaret Huddleston of Laprairie. (page 34)

Huddleston, Ellen

B-262, Ellen Huddleston, baptized 24 June 1866, daughter of Thomas and Margaret Huddleston of Laprairie. (page 33)

Huddleston, Henry

B-352, Henry Huddleston, baptized 17 October 1870, son of Adam and Rose Huddleston. (page 44)

Huddleston, Margaret Ann

B-263, Margaret Ann Huddleston, baptized 24 June 1866, daughter of Thomas and Margaret Huddleston of Laprairie. (page 33)

Huddleston, Mary Agnes

B-267, Mary Agnes Huddleston, baptized 24 June 1866, daughter of Thomas and Margaret Huddleston of Laprairie. (page 34)

Huddleston, Mary Jane

B-384, Mary Jane Huddleston, baptized 12 May 1872, daughter of Adam and Rose Huddleston. (page 48)

Huddleston, Rose

B-418, Rose Huddleston, baptized 18 October 1874, daughter of Adam and Rose Huddleston of Laprairie. (page 53)

Huddleston, Thomas

B-264, Thomas Huddleston, baptized 24 June 1866, son of Thomas and Margaret Huddleston of Laprairie. (page 33)

Huddlestone, Ada Louise

B-543, Ada Louise Huddlestone, born 5 March 1882, baptized 4 June 1882, daughter of Adam and Elizabeth Huddlestone of Portage la Prairie. (page 68)

Huddlestone, Adam and Elizabeth Victoria Huddlestone
M-96, Adam Huddlestone, age 40, widower, son of John Huddlestone, married 25 April 1881, Elizabeth Victoria Huddlestone, age 20, daughter of Thomas Huddlestone, by Henry George, Witness: John J. Setter. (page 49)

Huddlestone, Elizabeth Victoria
See Adam Huddlestone and Elizabeth Victoria Huddlestone

Huddlestone, Margaret Ann
S-172, Margaret Ann Huddleston, of Portage la Prairie, age 21 years 7 months, buried 1 March 1881. (page 22)

Huddlestone, Mary
S-136, Mary Huddlestone, of Portage la Prairie, age 7 years, buried 12 January 1878. (page 17)

Huddlestone, Rose
S-124, Rose Huddlestone, of Portage la Prairie, age 37, buried 16 April 1877. (page 16)

Hudlleston, Nancy Alice
B-347, Nancy Alice Huddleston, baptized 31 July 1870, daughter of Thomas and Margaret Huddleston. (page 44)

Hunt, Alice Elizabeth
S-146, Alice Elizabeth Hunt, of Burnside, age 12 years, buried 15 March 1879. (page 19)

Hunt, John
S-199, John Hunt, of Burnside, age 57, buried 31 December 1876. (page 15)

Indian
S-60, [no entry] (page 8)

Indian
S-71, [no entry] (page 9)

Indian
S-73, [no entry] (page 10)

Inkster, Duncan
B-195, Duncan Inkster, baptized 22 November 1863, son of Robert and Harriet Inkster of High Bluff. (page 25)

Inkster, Eliza

B-23, Eliza Inkster, baptized 30 October 1856, daughter of John and Isabella Inkster. (page 3)

Inkster, Elizabeth

S-15, Elizabeth Inkster [Isabelle Sanderson], of Portage la Prairie, age 45 years, buried 22 March 1860. (page 2)

Inkster, Isabella

See Alexander McLeod and Isabella Inkster

Inkster, James

B-28, James Inkster, baptized 17 May 1857, son of Robert and Harriet Inkster. (page 4)

Inkster, John

S-38, John Inkster, of Portage la Prairie, age 58 years, buried 2 August 1864. (page 5)

Inkster, Margaret

See William Sutherland and Margaret Inkster

Inkster, Mary

B-49, Mary Inkster, baptized [between 5 April and 19 June] 1859, daughter of Robert and Harriet Inkster. (page 7)

Inkster, Robert and Harriet Gill

M-2, Robert Inkster of Portage la Prairie, son of John Inkster, married 22 May 1856 Harriet Gill by Hellyer, Witnesses: Charles Whitford and Sarah Gill. (page 1)

Inkster, William Archibald

B-199, William Archibald Inkster, baptized 7 December 1863, son of James and Jane Inkster of Poplar Point. (page 25)

Inkster, William

B-110, William Inkster, baptized 8 September 1861, son of Robert and Harriet Inkster. (page 14)

Jackson, Andrew Clinton and Amelia Munro

M-6, Andrew Clinton Jacson, age 42, of Portage la Prairie, son of Thomas Jackson, married 20 January 1850, Amelia Munro, age 23, of Portage la Prairie, daughter of Hugh Munro, by William Cochran, Witnesses: Peter Garrioch and Frederick Bird. (page 3)

Jackson, Andrew J.

S-55, Andrew James Jackson, of Westbourne, age 12 weeks, buried 8 October 1866. (page 7)

Jackson, Andrew James

B-272, Andrew James Jackson, baptized 24 July 1866, son of Andrew and Amelie Jackson of Westbourne. (page 34)

Jacquish, Hiram and Nancy Corrigal

M-50, Hiram Jacquish, age 32, of St. Marys, married 1 April 1868, Nancy Corrigal, age 24, of St. Marys, daughter of James Corrigal, by Henry George, Witness: John Corrigal. (page 25)

Jaquish, Maria Catherine

B-356, Maria Catherine Jaquish, baptized 20 February 1871, daughter of Hiram and Nancy Jaquish of Laprairie. (page 45)

Jaquish, Mary Emma

B-326, Mary Emma D'Jaquish, baptized 25 April 1869, daughter of William and Nancy D'Jaquish, St. Marys. (page 41)

Jaquish, Roderick George

B-396, Roderick George Jaquish, baptized 13 April 1873, son of Hiram and Nancy Jaquish of White Mud River. (page 50)

Jemime, Adularde

S-167, Adularde Jemime, of Westbourne, age 2 years, buried 23 August 1880. (page 21)

Johnston, Anna Florence

B-551, Anna Florence Johnston, born 13 August 1882, daughter of John and Susan Johnston of Portage la Prairie. (page 69)

Johnston, James and Isabella Spence

M-32, James Johnston, age 18, of Westbourne, son of James Johnston, married 26 January 1865, Isabelle Spence, age 20, of Westbourne, daughter of Magnus Spence, by John Chapman, Witness: John Corrigal. (page 16)

Johnstone, Edward

B-362, Edward Johnstone, baptized 17 May 1871, son of James and Julia Johnstone of Laprairie. (page 46)

Johnstone, Elizabeth

B-261, Elizabeth Johnstone, baptized 22 May 1866, daughter of James and Isabelle Johnstone of Laprairie. (page 33)

Johnstone, Elizabeth

S-54, Elizabeth Johnstone of Portage la Prairie, age 5 weeks, buried 25 June 1866. (page 7)

Johnstone, Frances

B-453, Frances Johnstone, baptized 5 May 1877, daughter of James and Julia Johnstone of Portage la Prairie. (page 57)

Johnstone, Frances

S-161, Frances Johnston, of Portage la Prairie, age 3 years, buried 3 July 1880. (page 21)

Johnstone, Helen

B-424, Helen Johnstone, baptized 28 Mar 1874, daughter of James and Julia Johnstone of Laprairie. (page 53)

Johnstone, Isabelle

S-53, Isabelle Johnstone [Isabelle Spence], of Portage la Prairie, age 20 years, buried 8 June 1866. (page 7)

Johnstone, James and Julia Gibault

M-46, James Johnstone of Hudson Bay Company, of St. Marys, son of James Johnstone, married 7 November 1867, Julia Gibault, of St. Marys, by Henry George, Witnesses: Emma M. Bird, Ann E. Hodgson, Charles Anderson. (page 23)

Johnstone, James

S-125, James Johnstone, of Portage la Prairie, age __, buried 21 June 1877. (page 16)

Johnstone, James

S-4, James Johnstone, of Portage la Prairie, age _, buried 1 June 1857. (page 1)

Johnstone, Julia

S-156, Julia Johnstone, of Portage la Prairie, age 22 years, buried 7 June 1880. (page 20)

Johnstone, Maria

B-481, Maria Johnstone, baptized 15 May 1879, daughter of Julia Johnstone of Portage la Prairie. (page 61)

Johnstone, Mary Ann Jane

B-395, Mary Ann Jane Johnstone, baptized 29 Mar 1873, daughter of James and Julia Johnstone of Laprairie. (page 50)

Johnstone, William James

S-66, William James Johnstone of I. Settlement, age 1 year 9 months, buried 4 June 1868. (page 9)

Jones, John

B-161, John Jones, baptized 13 February 1863, son of John and Margaret Jones. (page 21)

Jordan, Ethel Clara

B-490, Ethel Clara Jordan, baptized 5 October 1879, daughter of George S. and Catherine Jordan (Engineer). (page 62)

Kelly, Robert

S-137, Robert Kelly, of Burnside, age 7 years and 8 months, buried 10 January 1878. (page 18)

Kenway, Parker Emuson

S-187, Parker Emuson Kenway, of Winnipeg, age 9 months, buried 9 September 1882. (page 24)

Kezinaugh, Joseph Jr. and Mary Todd

M-104, Joseph Kezinaugh Jr., age 19, of Portage la Prairie, son of Joseph Kezinaugh Sr., married 30 May 1883, Mary Todd, age 15, of Portage la Praire, daughter of William Todd and Elizabeth by A. C. Fortin. (page 53)

Kip, Elizabeth

B-165, Elizabeth Kip, baptized 29 March 1863, from Blackfoot Country. (page 21)

Kip, Elizabeth

See Robert Anderson and Elizabeth Kip

Knott, Joseph Albert

B-320, Joseph Albert Knott, [twin] baptized 27 December 1868, son of John and Mary Knott, St. Margarets, The Bluff. (page 40)

Knott, Mary Matilda

B-321, Mary Mathilda Knott, [twin] baptized 27 December 1868, daughter of John and Mary Knott, St. Margarets, The Bluff. (page 41)

Knott, Roderick

B-348, Roderick Knott, baptized 25 September 1870, son of Gavin and Hannah Knott of High Bluff. (page 44)

Lacorde, Sarah
> See Alexander McDonald and Sarah Lacorde

Leitch, Thomas Henry
> S-152, Thomas Henry Leitch, of Portage la Prairie, age 11 years, buried 11 November 1879. (page 19)

Levesconte, Charles James
> S-139, Charles James Levesconte, of Portage la Prairie, from Campbell, Ontario, age 23 years, buried 18 June 1878. (page 18)

Lewis, Robert
> S-132, Robert Lewis, of Portage la Prairie, age 37 years, buried 17 November 1877. (page 17)

Lyall, Mabel
> B-586, Mabel F. Lyall, baptized 9 December 1883, daughter of William and Emily Helen Lyall. (page 74)

Lyons, William James
> B-415, William James Lyons, baptized 19 July 1874, son of William and Jane Lyons. (page 52)

MacDonald, Donald and Margaret Ann McDonald
> M-74, Donald MacDonald, age 25, of Portage Creek, son of Edward MacDonald, married 6 August 1874, Margaret Ann McDonald, age 25, of Portage Creek, daughter of James MacDonald, by Henry George, Witnesses: Donald MacDonald and Edward MacDonald. (page 37)

Mackay, George Alexander
> B-115, George Alexander Mackay, baptized 13 October 1862, son of John Dougal and Harriet Mackay. (page 15)

Mackay, Julia
> B-154, Julia Mackay, baptized 14 December 1862, daughter of John Dougal and Harriet Mackay. (page 20)

Mackay, Kezia
> B-97, Kezia Mackay, baptized 28 April 1861, daughter of William and Susanah (Hunter). (page 13)

Mair, Ada Amanda
> See John Anderson and Ada Amanda Mair

Matheson, Alexy

See John Corrigal and Alexy Matheson

Mathews, Hugh

S-170, Hugh Mathews, of Portage la Prairie, age 67 years, buried 31 December 1880. (page 22)

Mathews, Thomas and Susan Laplante

M-31, Thomas Mathews, age 21, of Laprairie, son of John Mathews, married 26 January 1865, Susan Laplante, age 22 daughter of S. Laplante, by William Cochran, Witnesses: William Norn and Donald Whitford. (page 16)

Maxwell, Agnes Louisa

B-449, Agnes Louisa Maxwell, baptized 28 January 1877, daughter of Andrew and Flora Maxwell, of Portage la Prairie. (page 57)

Maxwell, Andrew and Flora Garrioch

M-79, Andrew Maxwell, age 35, of Portage la Prairie, son of Edward Maxwell, married 9 December 1875, Flora Garrioch, age 20, of Portage la Prairie, daughter of John Garrioch, by Henry George, Witness: R. Howard. (page 40)

Maxwell, Colin James Edward

B-469, Colin James Edward Maxwell, baptized 25 August 1878, son of Andrew and Flora Maxwell. (page 59)

McBain, Margaret

See Farquhar McLean and Margaret McBain

McCorrister, Alexander James

B-226, Alexander James McCorrister (adopted), baptized 5 June 1864, son of James and Sarah McCorrister of Poplar Point. (page 29)

McCulloch, Jacob James

B-489, Jacob James McCulloch, baptized 288 September 1879, son of William and Anne McCulloch. (page 62)

McCulloch, Margaret Ann

S-134, Margaret Ann McCulloch, of Portage la Prairie, age 11-1/2 years, buried 25 December 1877. (page 17)

McCulloch, Mary Jane

B-461, Mary Jane McCulloch, baptized 25 December 1877, William and Ann McCulloch of Portage la Prairie. (page 58)

McCulloch, Mary Jane

S-135, Mary Jane McCulloch, of Portage la Prairie, age 1 year 11 months, buried 2 January 1878. (page 17)

McDonald, Alexander and Sarah Lacorde

M-55, Alexander McDonald, age 40, of St. Marys, married 2 May 1870, Sarah Lacorde, age 25, widow, of St. Marys, daughter of Lightning, by Henry George, Witnesses: Charles Cummings and Thomas Corrigal. (page 28)

McDonald, Annie

B-334, Annie McDonald, baptized 1 December 1869, daughter of William and Christina McDonald. (page 42) The scrip application states this date is in error.

McDonald, Annie

S-120, Annie McDonald, of Portage la Prairie, age 6-1/2 years, buried 3 June 1877. (page 15)

McDonald, Christiane

S-113, Christiane McDonald, daughter of Alexander and Sarah McDonald, of Portage la Prairie, age 1 year 8 months, buried 8 October 1875. (page 15)

McDonald, Christina

B-407, Christina McDonald, baptized 29 March 1874, daughter of Alexander and Sarah McDonald of Laprairie. (page 51)

McDonald, Christine

S-122, Christiana McDonald, of Portage la Prairie, age 30, buried 30 March 1877. (page 16)

McDonald, Elizabeth

B-442, Elizabeth McDonald, baptized 9 July 1876, daughter of Alexander and Sarah McDonald of Laprairie. (page 56)

McDonald, Margaret Ann

See Donald MacDonald and Margaret Ann McDonald

McDonald, Mary Catherine

B-358, Mary Catherine McDonald, baptized 17 March 1871, daughter of Alexander and Sarah McDonald of Laprairie. (page 45)

McDonald, Mary Catherine

S-78, Mary Catherine McDonald, of Portage la Prairie, age 1 months, buried 19 April 1871. (page 10)

McDonald, Mary Jane Adeline

B-534, Mary Jane Adeline McDonald, born 15 September 1881, daughter of William and Armeline McDonald of Portage la Prairie. (page 67)

McDonald, Sarah Ann

B-380, Sarah Ann McDonald, baptized 14 April 1873, daughter of Alex and Sarah McDonald of Laprairie. (page 48)

McDonald, Sarah

S-121, Sarah McDonald, of Portage la Prairie, age 26, buried, 21 February 1877, (page 16)

McDonald, Susan

B-436, Susan McDonald, baptized 28 Januar 1876, daughter of William and Christiana McDonald of Laprairie. (page 55)

McDonald, William Alexander

B-403, William Alexander McDonald, baptized 21 December 1873, son of William and Christiana McDonald of Laprairie. (page 51)

McDonald, William and Christiana McKay

M-41, William McDonald, age 28, of St.Johns, son of Neil McDonald, married 16 May 1867, Christiann McKay, age 20, of St. Marys, daughter of William McKay, by Henry George, Witnesses: William McKay, Joseph McKay and William Henderson. (page 21)

McDonald, William McKay

B-372, William McKay McDonald, baptized 24 December 1871, son of William and Christiana McDonald of Laprairie. (page 47)

McDougall, Isabelle

S-112, Isabelle McDougall, of Lake Manitoba, age 30 years, buried 30 October 1876. (page 14)

McIver, Catherine

See Edward Field and Catherine McIver

McIver, Christia Bella

B-317, Christie Bella McIver, baptized 20 September 1868, daughter of Allen and Elizabeth McIver, Portage la Prairie, HBC servant. (page 40)

McIver, Elizabeth

B-90, Elizabeth McIver, baptized 12 January 1861, daughter of Allen and Elizabeth McIver. (page 12)

McIver, Elizabeth

S-105, Elizabeth McIver [Elizabeth Beeds], wife of Allen McIver, of Westbourne, age 41, buried 19 November 1874. (page 14)

McIver, John Henry

B-204, John Henry McIver, baptized 13 January 1864, son of Allen and Ellen McIver. (page 26)

McIver, Mary Margaret

See John Daniel and Mary Margaret McIver

McKay, Absolom Etienne

S-93, Absolom E. McKay, of Parmetheon Hills, age 19 years 5 months, buried 1 May 1873. (page 12)

McKay, Christiana

See William McDonald and Christiana McKay

McKay, Edward Archibald

B-416, Edward Archibald McKay, baptized 19 July 1874, son of John D. and Harriet McKay of Laprairie. (page 52)

McKay, Flora

B-350, Flora McKay, baptized 2 October 1870, daughter of William McKay and Susannah of Laprairie. (page 44)

McKay, Florence Louisa

S-142, Florence Louisa McKay, of Portage la Prairie, age 1 year 2 months, buried 27 August 1878. (page 18)

McKay, Francis

B-337, Francis McKay, baptized 27 March 1870, son of John D. and Harriet McKay. (page 43)

McKay, George Alexander

S-20, George Alexander McKay, of Portage la Prairie, age 5 months, buried 1 February 1862. (page 3)

McKay, Gertrude Jane

B-485, Gertrude Jane McKay, baptized 13 July 1879, daughter of John D. and Harriet McKay of Portage la Prairie. (page 61)

McKay, Harriet Ann

B-383, Harriet Ann McKay, baptized 12 May 1872, daughter of William D. and Harriet McKay. (page 48)

McKay, Henry

B-305, Henry McKay, baptized 18 January 1868, son of John D. and Harriet McKay, St. Marys, HBC servant. (page 39)

McKay, John James

B-239, John James McKay, baptized 13 April 1865, son of John Dougal and Harriet McKay of Laprairie. (page 30)

McKay, John James

S-115, John James McKay, son of John Dougall McKay of Portage la Prairie, age 10 years, buried 15 November 1875. (page 15)

McKay, Joseph

S-89, Joseph McKay of Fort Ellice, age 22 years, buried 28 November 1872. (page 12)

McKay, Julia

See James Cusitor and Julia McKay

McKay, Louisa Florence

B-456, Louise Florence McKay, baptized 26 August 1877, daughter of John D. and Harriet McKay of Portage la Prairie. (page 57)

McKay, Martha

B-313, Martha McKay, baptized 14 June 1868, daughter of William and Susannah McKay, St. Marys. (page 40)

McKay, Martha

S-74, Martha McKay, of Portage la Prairie, age 8 months, buried 11 February 1869. (page 10)

McKay, Micha

B-259, Micha McKay, baptized 5 March 1866, daughter of William and Susannah McKay of Portage la Prairie. (page 33)

McKenzie, Catherine

B-229, Catherine McKenzie, baptized 24 July 1864, daughter of Benjamin and Harriet McKenzie of Laprairie. (page 29)

McKenzie, Eliza

B-85, Eliza McKenzie, baptized 21 October 1860, daughter of Benjmain and Harriet McKenzie. (page 11)

McKenzie, Hugh and Mary Ann McLean

M-86, Hugh McKenzie, age 18, of La Praire, son of Hector McKenzie, married 19 July 1878, Mary Ann McLennan, age 18, of Portage la Prairie, daughter of Murdoch McLennan, by Henry George, Witnesses: Murdoch McKenzie, Margaret McLennan. (page 44)

McLean, Clementine

See Robert Wishart and Clementine McLean

McLean, Ellen

B-23, Ellen McLean, baptized 1 January 1865, daughter of Farquhar and Margaret McLean of Laprairie. (page 30)

McLean, Ellen

S-56, Ellen McLean of La Prairie, age 1 year and 11 months, buried 19 October 1866. (page 7)

McLean, Farquhar and Margaret McBain

M-29, Farquhar McLean, age 27, of Laprairie, son of Donald McLean, married 3 December 1863, Margret McBain, age 17, of Laprairie, daughter of Kenneth McBain, by Thomas Cochrane, Witnesses: Clementine McLean and William Tait. (page 15)

McLean, Hugh

B-276, Hugh McLean, baptized 13 July 1866, child of Farquhar and Margaret McLean of Laprairie. (page 35)

McLean, Mary Ann

See Hugh McKenzie and Mary Ann McLean

McLeod, Alexander and Isabella Inkster

M-28, Alexander McLeod, age 22, High Bluff, son of Donald McLeod, married 21 September 1863, Isabelle Inkster, age 16, of High Bluff, daughter of John Inkster, by Wm. Cochrane, Witnesses: Peter Henderson and Alexander Taylor. (page 14)

McNab, Andrew James

B-158, Andrew James McNab, baptized [between 11 January and 8 February] 1863, son of James and Catherine McNab of Poplar Point. (page 20)

McNab, James

B-129, James McNab, baptized 9 February 1862, son of John and Mary McNab of Poplar Point. (page 17)

McNab, John Thomas

B-98, John Thomas McNab, baptized 28 April 1861, son of James and Catherine McNab of Poplar Point. (page 13)

McNab, Margaret L.

B-225, Margaret L. McNab, baptized 5 June 1864, daughter of John and Mary McNab of Poplar Point. (page 29)

McPhail, Harriet

B-171, Harriet McPhail, baptized 26 April 1863, daughter of Duncan and Mathilda McPhail in Hudson Bay Company service. (page 22)

McVicar, John and Mary Harriet Garrioch

M-73, John McVicar, age 27, of Winnipeg, son of Duncan McVicar, married 9 May 1872, Mary Harriet Garrioch, age 18, of Portage la Prairie, daughter of John Garrioch, by Henry George, Witness: John James Setter. (page 34)

Merrick, Ethel Victoria

B-580, Ethel Victoria Merrick, baptized 12 August 1883, daughter of William and Emma Mary Merrick. (page 73)

Miller, Bernard West

B-502, Bernard West Miller, baptized 10 July 1880, son of Francis Benjamin and Fanny Miller (Birtle, Manitoba). (page 63)

Miller, Dorothy

B-503, Dorothy Miller, baptized 10 July 1880, daughter of Francis Benjamin and Fanny Miller (Birtle, Manitoba). (page 63)

Miller, Dorothy

S-168, Dorothy Miller, of Birtle, Manitoba, age 2 months 8 days, buried 24 August 1880. (page 21)

Miller, Gertrude

B-443, Gertrude Miller, baptized 14 August 1876, daughter of Augustus and Ann Miller of Westbourne. (page 56)

Miller, Richard Huntuy

S-138, Richard Huntuay Miller, of Portage la Prairie, age 7 days, buried 17 June 1878. (page 18)

Mills, Mary M.

B-486, Mary M. Mills, baptized 7 September 1879, daughter of Augustus and Anne Mills of Portage la Prairie. (page 61)

Mills, Richard Hunter

B-467, Richard Hunter Mills, baptized 14 June 1878, son of Augustus and Ann Mills, of Portage la Prairie. (page 59)

Mills, Walter Reginald

B-515, Walter Reginald Mills, born 15 February 1881, baptized 18 June 1881, son of Augustus and Anne Mills of Swan River, NWT. (page 65)

Moffat, Elizabeth

See Johnny Scott and Elizabeth Moffat

Moffat, Susan

See Joseph Corrigal and Susan Moffat

Monkman, Alexander

B-341, Alexander Monkman, baptized 15 May 1870, son of Henry and Nancy Monkman. (page 43)

Monkman, Henry and Nancy Spence

M-48, Henry Monkman, age 30, widower, of Manitoba District, son of James Monkman, married 27 February 1868, Nancy Spence, age 28, widow, of St. Marys, daughter of Peter Whitford, by Henry George, Witness: Elizabeth Jane Cook. (page 24)

Moosoo, Basil and Catherine Anderson

M-17, Basil Moosoo, age 35 of Laprairie, son of Basil Moosoo, married 12 September 1861, Catherine Anderson, and 29, of Laprairie, daughter of Thomas Anderson, by Thos. Cochrane, Witnesses: Joseph A. Turner, Alexander Whitford. (page 9)

Moosoo, Catherine

See Samuel Spence and Catherine Moosoo

Moosoo, Mary

S-96, Mary Moosoo, of Portage la Prairie, age 16 months, buried 1 September 1873. (page 12)

Morrias, Antoine

S-7, Antoine Morrias, of Portage la Prairie, age 2 months, buried 24 December 1857. (page 1)

Mortiz, __

[no entry] (page 20)

Mowat, Ida

See Peter George and Ida Mowat

Muir, Fanny George

B-402, Fanny George Muir, baptized 21 December 1873, daughter of Charles and Eliza Muir of Laprairie. (page 51)

Muir, Florence Margaret Holmes

B-377, Marie Florence Margaret Holmes Muir, baptized 24 March 1872, daughter of Charles Muir and Louisa, of Laprairie. (page 48)

Muir, George Denison

B-434, George Denison Muir, baptized 6 December 1875, son of Charles and Eliza Muir of Laprairie. (page 55)

Munro, Amelia

See Andrew Clinton Jackson and Amelia Munro

Nelson, Julia

See Samuel Carpenter and Julia Nelson

Newall, Edwin Edward and Jane Donely

M-72, Edwin Edward Newall, age 28 of LaPrairie, son of Joseph Newall, married 4 November 1873, Jane Donely, age 18, of LaPrairie, daughter of William Donley, by Henry George. (page 36)

Newell, Edith Mary

B-421, Edith Mary Newell, baptized 15 November 1874, daughter of Edward Edwin and Jane Newell of Laprairie. (page 53)

Norn, Adeline

B-160, Adeline Norn, baptized 8 February 1863, daughter of William and Sarah Norn. (page 20)

Norn, Ann

B-47, Ann Norn, baptized 20 March 1859, daughter of William and Sophia Norn. (page 6)

Norn, Joseph Alexander

B-95, Joseph Alexander Norn, baptized 3 March 1861, son of William and Sarah Norn. (page 12)

Norn, Mary Elizabeth

B-29, Mary Elizabeth Norn, baptized 24 May 1857, daughter of William and Sarah Norn. (page 4)

Norn, Thomas

B-230, Thomas Norn, baptized 26 September 1864, son of William and Sarah Norn of Laprairie. (page 29)

Norquay, Alexander

B-299, Alexander Norquay, baptized 1 December 1867, son of John and Elizabeth Norquay, St. Margarets, P.L.P. (page 38)

Norquay, James

B-88, James Norquay, baptized 3 January 1861, son of John and Mary Norquay of Poplar Point. (page 11)

Norquay, John and Mary Sandison

M-13, John Norquay, age 22, of Laprairie, son of Henry Norquay, married 2 February 1860, Mary Sandison, age 20 of Laprairie, daughter of James Sandison. (page 7)

Norquay, John and Elizabeth Setter

M-20, John Norquay, age 21, of St.Andrews, married 2 January 1862, Elizabeth Setter, age 19, of Laprairie, daughter of George Setter, by Thomas Cochrane, Witnesses: John James Setter and Alexander McBeth. (page 10)

Norquay, Maria

B-207, Maria Norquay, baptized 9 February 1864, daughter of John and Mary Norquay. (page 26)

Norquay, Mary Harriet

B-302, Mary Harriet Norquay, baptized 24 December 1867, daughter of John and Mary Norquay, St. Margarets. (page 38)

Otton, Frances Waster

S-166, Frances Waster Otton, of Lake Manitoba, age 5 years, buried 21 August 1880. (page 21)

Otton, Fred Alf

S-165, Fred Alf Otton, of Lake Manitoba, age 5 years, buried 19 August 1880. (page 21)

Palmer, Lewis Allan

S-158, Lewis Allan Palmer, of Portage la Prairie, age 6-1/2 years, buried 15 June 1880. (page 20)

Palmer, Nelly May

S-157, Nelly May Palmer, of Portage la Prairie, age 3 years, buried 8 June 1880. (page 20)

Park, James and Mary Gibeau

M-88, James Park, age 25, of Portage la Prairie, married 31 July 1878, Mary Gibeau, age 17, of Portage la Prairie, by Henry George. (page 44)

Park, James

S-159, James Park, of Portage la Prairie, age 30 years, buried 25 June 1880. (page 20)

Parker, Elias Ernest

B-509, Elias Ernest Parker, baptized 27 December 1880, son of John and Elizabeth Parker of Portage la Prairie. (page 64)

Parker, George Alfred

S-145, George Alfred Parker, of Portage la Prairie, age 10 months 3 weeks, buried 7 February 1879. (page 19)

Parker, Mary J.

See James Edward George and Mary J. Parker

Parker, Nellie

B-573, Nellie May Parker, baptized 25 June 1883, daughter of John and Elizabeth Parker. (page 72)

Pelham, Charles

B-150, Charles Pelham, baptized 27 November 1862, son of Peter and Mary Pelham. (page 19)

Pelham, Margaret

B-151, Margaret Pelham, baptized 27 November 1862, daughter of Peter and Mary Pelham. (page 19)

Pelham, Mary Ann

B-149, Mary Ann Pelham, baptized 27 November 1862, daughter of Peter and Mary Pelham. (page 19)

Pelham, Mary

B-148, Mary Pelham, baptized 27 November 1862 (adult Indian). (page 19)

Pelham, Mary

S-24, Mary Pelham, of Portage la Prairie, age 17 years, buried 4 August 1863. (page 3)

Pelham, Peter

B-147, Peter Pelham, baptized 27 November 1862 (adult Indian). (page 19)

Pelham, Peter

S-25, Peter Pelham, of Portage la Prairie, age 40 years, buried 4 August 1863. (page 4)

Pelly, Edward and Ellen Garrioch

M-80, Edward Pelly, age 26, of Portage la Prairie, son of Charles Pelly, married 22 March 1875, Ellen Garrioch, age 18, of Portage la Prairie, daughter of John Garrioch, by Henry George. (page 41)

Pelly, Ina Rosalie

B-447, Ina Rosalie Pelly, baptized 26 November 1876, daughter of Edward and Ellen Pelly of Laprairie. (page 56)

Pelly, John Harold

S-153, John Harold Pelly, of Portage la Prairie, age 5-1/2 months, buried 6 January 1880. (page 20)

Pelly, John Harold

B-488, John Harold Pelly, baptized 28 September 1879, son of Edward and Ellen Pelly of Portage la Prairie. (page 61)

Pelly, Percy Bertram

B-468, Percy Bertram Pelly, baptized 23 June 1878, son of Edward and Ellen Pelly of Portage la Prairie. (page 59)

Peterson, Andrew and Mary Ann Erasmus
M-23, Andrew Peterson, of Poplar Bluff, married 27 November 1862, Mary Ann Erasmus of Poplar Bluff, daughter of Peter Erasmus, by William Cochran, Witnesses: J. Finlay Wray and William Clark. (page 12)

Peterson, Augusta
B-187, Augusta Peterson, baptized 11 October 1863, daughter of Andrew and Mary Peterson. (page 24)

Peterson, Ray
B-306, Ray Peterson, baptized 19 January 1868, son of Andrew and Mary Anne Peterson of St. Margarets. (page 39)

Plummer, Charlotte Elizabeth
B-557, Charlotte Elizabeth Plummer, baptized [?] 8 November 1882, daughter of Thomas and Charlotte Plummer of Portage la Prairie. (page 70)

Pocha, Catherine
B-281, Catherine Pocha, baptized 3 February 1867, daughter of William and Maria Pocha, of St.Margaret Parish. (page 36)

Pocha, Catherine
See Francis Desmarais and Catherine Pocha

Pocha, Charles and Mary Ann Tate
M-47, Charles Pocha, age 27, of St. Margarets, son of Joseph Pocha, married 16 January 1868, Mary Ann Tate, age 20, of St. Margarets, daughter of Joseph Tate, Witnesses: Eliza Adams and James Mulligan. (page 24)

Pocha, Charlotte
B-185, Charlotte Pocha, baptized 4 October 1863, daughter of Joseph and Mathilda Pocha of High Bluff. (page 24)

Pocha, Elizabeth
B-55, Elizabeth Pocha, baptized 5 August 1859, daughter of Joseph and Mary Pocha. (page 7)

Pocha, Fanny
See Thomas and Anderson Fanny Pocha

Pocha, Harriet
B-318, Harriet Pocha, baptized 11 October 1868, daughter of William and Marie Pocha, St. Margarets, High Bluff. (page 40)

Pocha, John James

B-83, John James Pocha, baptized 23 September 1860, son of Joseph and Mathla Pocha. (page 11)

Pocha, John James

B-57, John James Pocha, baptized 28 August 1859, son of John and Harriet Pocha. (page 8)

Pocha, Joseph and Matilda Hodgson

M-12, Joseph Pocha, age 27, of Laprairie, son of Joseph Pocha, married 29 November 1859, Matilda Hodgson, age 28, daughter of John Hodgson, by William Cochran, Witnesses: John Hodgson and William Pocha. (page 6)

Pocha, Joseph

B-124, Joseph Pocha, baptized 19 January 1862, son of Joseph and Mathilda Pocha of High Bluff. (page 16)

Pocha, Maria

B-293, Maria Pocha, baptized 11 August 1867, daughter of Joseph and Matilda Pocha, St.Margaret (P.L.P.). (page 37)

Pocha, Mary

B-172, Mary Pocha, baptized 26 April 1863, daughter of John and Harriet Pocha of High Bluff. (page 22)

Pocha, Mary

S-36, Mary Pocha, of High Bluff, age 10 years, buried 9 May 1864. (page 5)

Pocha, William and Maria Anderson

M-35, William Pocha, age 25, of St. Margarets, son of Joseph Pocha, married 23 November 1865, Maria Anderson, age 18, of St. Marys Parish, daughter of Thomas Anderson, by Henry George, Witnesses: Joseph Adams, Charles Pocha, Robert Adams, Joe Pocha, Tom Anderson. (page 18)

Pratt, Mary Blanche

S-164, Mary Blanche Pratt, of Portage la Prairie, age 13 months 5 days, buried 17 August 1880. (page 21)

Pratt, Mary Blanche

B-487, Mary Blanche Pratt, baptized 7 September 1879, daughter of Walter and Elizabeth Pratt of Laprairie. (page 61)

Pratt, Rosalind

B-508, Rosalind Pratt, baptized 20 December 1880, daughter of Walter and Elizabeth Ann Pratt of Portage la Prairie. (page 64)

Pratt, Rosalind

S-169, Rosalind Pratt, of Portage la Prairie, age 9 days, buried 30 December 1880. (page 22)

Pratt, Walter M. and Elizabeth Ann George

M-85, Walter M. Prate, age 24, of Westbourne, son of J. Prate, married 8, June 1878, Elizabeth Ann George, age 21, of Portage la Prairie, daughter of Henry George, by Henry George, Witnesses: Donald Pratt, Richard Byers. (page 43)

Prince, Anna Belle

S-184, Anna Belle Prince, of Long Plains, age 7 years, buried 17 April 1882. (page 23)

Prince, Edward George

B-454, Edward George Prince, baptized 7 June 1877, son of Peter and Sarah Prince of Portage la Prairie. (page 57)

Prince, Edward George

S-143, Edward George Prince, of Portage la Prairie, age 1 year 3 months, buried 25 August 1878. (page 18)

Prince, John Henry

B-484, John Henry Prince, baptized 29 Jun 1879, son of Peter and Sarah Prince of Portage la Prairie. (page 61)

Prince, Maggie

S-180, Maggie Prince, of Portage la Prairie, age __, buried 27 February 1882. (page 23)

Prince, Peter and Sarah Helena Anderson

M-62, Peter Prince, age 18, of Westbourne, married [between 10 May 1871 and 15 June 1871], Sarah Helena Anderson of same place. (page 31)

Richard, John

S-75, John Richard, of Portage la Prairie, age 8 months, buried 3 May 1869. (page 10)

Richard, Joseph

B-178, Joseph Richard, baptized 28 June 1863, son of Francois and Mary Richard of High Bluff. (page 23)

Robertson, Emma
S-190, Emma Robertson, of Portage la Prairie, age 28 years, buried 29 March 1883. (page 24)

Robertson, Jane
B-270, Jane Robertson, baptized 6 July 1866, daughter of George and Victoria Robertson of Long Lake. (page 34)

Robinson, Agnes
B-585, Agnes Robinson, baptized 11 November 1883, daughter of Charles and Agnes Robinson of Portage la Prairie. (page 74)

Robinson, Jane
B-180, Jane Robinson, baptized 23 Aug 1863, daughter of William and Frances Robinson. (page 23)

Ross, Charles Edward
B-558, Charles Edward Ross, born 20 November 1882, son of Benjamin Charles and Maggie Jane Ross of Winnipeg. (page 558)

Rutledge, Janet
S-95, Janet Rutledge, of Rate Creek, age 40 years, buried 27 August 1873. (page 12)

Sanderson, Alexander and Maria Henderson
M-63, Alexander Sanderson, age 21, of St.Andrews; married 15 June 1871, Maria Henderson, age 20, of St. Marys, daughter of Peter Henderson, by Henry George, Witnesses: Charles Henderson, Dan McLeod, Margaret Henderson. (page 32)

Sanderson, Alexander
B-550, Alexander Sanderson, born 3 August 1882, son of Alexander and Maria Sanderson of Portage la Prairie. (page 69)

Sanderson, Annabella
B-103, Annabella Sanderson, baptized 30 January 1861, daughter of George and Mary Sanderson, of Hudson Bay Company Fort Ellice. (page 13)

Sanderson, Colin
B-301, Colin Sanderson, baptized 27 October 1867, son of Thomas and Sarah Sanderson, St. Margarets. (page 38)

Sanderson, Elizabeth Jane
B-381, Elizabeth Jane Sanderson, baptized 14 April 1872, daughter of Alex and Marie Sanderson of Laprairie. (page 48)

Sanderson, Elizabeth Jane

S-174, Elizabeth Jane Sanderson, of Portage la Prairie, age 9 years, buried 20 March 1881. (page 22)

Sanderson, Henry George

B-410, Henry George Sanderson, baptized 10 May 1874, son of Alex and Maria Sanderson of Laprairie. (page 52)

Sanderson, Isabella Ann

B-507, Isabella Ann Sanderson, baptized 19 December 1880, daughter of Alexander and Mary Sanderson of Portage la Prairie. (page 64)

Sanderson, Margaret Harriet

B-102, Margaret Harriet Sanderson, baptized 30 June 1861, daughter of George and Mary Sanderson, of Hudson Bay Company Fort Ellice. (page 13)

Sanderson, Robert James

B-63, Robert James Sandison, baptized 22 November 1859, son of Thomas and Sarah Sandison. (page 8)

Sanderson, Robert James

S-85, Robert James Sanderson, of Portage la Prairie, age 12 years, buried 19 November 1871. (page 11)

Sanderson, William

B-474, William Sanderson, baptized 15 December 1878, son of Alexander and Marie Sanderson of Laprairie. (page 60)

Sandison, Benjamin

B-375, Benjamin Sandison, baptized 17 March 1872, son of Thomas and Sarah Sandison of Laprairie. (page 47)

Sandison, Catherine

B-220, Catherine Sandison (adopted), baptized 16 March 1864, daughter of David and Mary Sandison of High Bluff. (page 28)

Sandison, Henry George

B-106, Henry George Sandison, baptized 14 August 1861, son of Thomas and Sarah Sandison. (page 14)

Sandison, Jane
   B-157, Jane Sandison, baptized 11 January 1863, daughter of William and Mary Sandison of Poplar Point. (page 20)

Sandison, Mary
   See John Norquay and Mary Sandison

Sandison, Thomas and Sarah Gill
   M-7, Thomas Sandison, age 27, of Laprairie, son of an Indian, married 3 February 1859, Sarah Gill, age 18, by William Cochran, Witnesses: Charles Anderson and Henry Laronde. (page 4)

Sandison, William
   B-181, William Sandison, baptized 23 August 1863, son of Thomas and Sarah Sandison. (page 23)

Sandison, William
   B-24, William Sandison, baptized 23 November 1856, son of George and Mary Sandison. (page 3)

Scarrow, Francis and Catherine Cavanaugh
   M-90, Francis Scarrow, age 28 of Winnipeg, son of William Scarrow, married 29 September 1880, Catherine Cavanaugh, of Portage la Prairie, daughter of __ Cavanaugh, by Henry George. (page 46)

Scott, Johnny and Elizabeth Moffat
   M-76, Johnny Scott, widower, of Portage la Prairie, son of John Scott, married 30 March 1875, Elizabeth Scott, of Portage la Prairie, daughter of James Moffat, by Henry George, Witnesses: Susan Moffat and Joseph Corrigal. (page 39)

Scott, Margaret Rebecca
   S-94, Margaret Rebecca Scott, of Portage la Prairie, age 27 years, buried 22 June 1873. (page 12)

Scott, Rebecca
   S-88, Rebecca Scott, of Portage la Prairie, age 9 months, buried 18 July 1872. (page 11)

Sellick, David William
   B-545, David William Sellick born 31 July 1882, son of Robert and Eman Sellick of Portage la Prairie. (page 69)

Setter, Alexander Andrew

B-228, Alexander Andrew Setter, baptized 4 July 1864, son of John James and Ann Setter of Laprairie. (page 29)

Setter, Alexander Andrew

S-42, Alexander Andrew Setter, of Portage la Prairie, age 5 months, buried 16 November 1864. (page 6)

Setter, Christiana Isabella

B-308, Christiana Isabella Setter, baptized 9 March 1868, daughter of John James and Ann Setter, St. Marys, school teacher. (page 39)

Setter, Elizabeth

See John Norquay and Elizabeth Setter

Setter, Hugh George

B-153, Hugh George Setter, baptized 12 December 1862, son of John James and Ann Setter. (page 20)

Setter, Hugh George

S-37, Hugh George Setter of Portage la Prairie, age 1 year and 5 months, buried 13 May 1864. (page 5)

Setter, James Cowan

B-446, James Cowan Setter, baptized 26 November 1876, son of John James and Anne Setter of Deputy Siding. (page 56)

Setter, James Cowan

S-160, James Cowan Setter, of Portage la Prairie, age 3 years, buried 3 July 1880. (page 20)

Setter, Maurice Charles

B-257, Maurice Charles Setter, baptized 25 February 1866, son of John James and Ann Setter school teacher of Portage la Prairie. (page 33)

Setter, Olivier

B-217, Oliver Setter, baptized 9 March 1864, son of John and Eliza Setter of Poplar Point. (page 28)

Simpson, David and Margaret Favel

B-34, David Simpson, age 25, of Laprairie, son of Thomas Simpson, married 26 January 1865, Margaret Favel, age 17, of Touchwood Hills, daughter of Richard Favel, by John Chapman, Witnesses: Richard Favel, Bill Favel. (page 17)

Sinclair, Flora Bell

B-390, Flora Bell Sinclair, baptized 10 September 1872, daughter of Thomas and Lizette Sinclair of Touchwood Hills. (page 49)

Sinclair, George

S-132, George Sinclair (Sioux child), of Portage la Prairie, age 5 months, buried 7 July 1877. (page 16)

Sinclair, James

S-58, James Sinclair, of La Prairie and the H.B.Co., age 40, buried 15 February 1867. (page 8)

Sinclair, William Thomas

B-56, William Thomas Sinclair, baptized 15 August 1859, son of Thomas and Lizette Sinclair. (page 7)

Smith, David George

B-571, David George Smith, baptized 24 June 1883, son of Thomas James and Anne Smith. (page 72)

Smith, Elizabeth

B-116, Elizabeth Smith, baptized 25 October 1862, daughter of Thomas Smith and a Heathen woman. (page 15)

Smith, Isabel Dorothy

See William Byers and Isabel Dorothy Smith

Smith, Isabella

B-155, Isabella Smith, baptized 25 December 1862, daughter of Angus and Mary Smith of High Bluff. (page 20)

Smith, John

B-235, John Smith, baptized 1 January 1865, son of James and Nancy Smith of Laprairie. (page 30)

Smith, Leslie

B-517, Leslie Smith, born 8 February 1881, baptized 21 June 1881, child of William Peter and Charlotte Smith. (page 65)

Smith, Maggie Maude

B-505, Maggie Maude Smith, baptized 15 September 1880, daughter of James and Margaret Smith of Portage la Prairie. (page 64)

Smith, Maggie

S-182, Maggie Smith, of Portage la Prairie, age 25 years 8 months, buried 10 March 1882. (page 23)

Smith, Samuel and Mary Ann Desmarais

M-39, Samuel Smith, age 18, of St.Andrews, son of John James Smith, married 14 February 1867, Mary Ann Desmarais, age 17 of St. Margarets High Bluff, daughter of Baptiste Desmarais, by Henry George, Witnesses: Robert Cook, Maria Halcrow, Peter Henderson, and John Corrigal. (page 20)

Smith, Thomas James and Annie Cusitor

M-99, Thomas James Smith, age 32, of Portage la Prairie, son of Thomas James Smith, married 6 June 1882, Annie Cusitor, age 22, of Portage la Prairie, daughter of David Cusitor, by Henry George. (page 50)

Smith, William James Cowan

B-494, William James Cowan Smith, baptized 14 March 1880, son of William and Margaret Smith. (page 62)

Smith,Charles Ernest

B-570, Charles Ernest Smith, baptized 21 June 1885, son of William Peter and Charlotte Smith. (page 72)

Spence, Alfred

B-94, Alfred Spence, baptized 28 February 1861, son of Joseph and Janet Spence. (page 12)

Spence, Andrew and Ann Whitford

M-33, Andrew Spence, age 23, of Laprairie, son of Magnus Spence, married 26 January 1865, Ann Whitford, age 18, of Laprairie, daughter of James Whitford, by John Chapman, Witnesses: Peter Henderson and John Corrigal. (page 17)

Spence, Archibald

B-370, Archibald Spence, baptized 26 July 1871, son of Nicol and Sohia Spence of Westbourne. (page 47)

Spence, David

B-246, David Spence, baptized 4 June 1865, son of Nicol and Sophia Spence, Fisherman at Westbourne. (page 31)

Spence, Edwin and Jemima Cusitor

M-100, Edwin Spence, age 21, of High Bluff, son of Andrew Spence, married 6 June 1882, Jemima Cusitor, age 18, of Portage la Prairie, daughter of David Cusitor, by A. Fortin, Witnesses: George Spence and T. J. Smith. (page 51)

Spence, Elizabeth

S-17, Elizabeth Spence, of Portage la Prairie, age 2 years and 8 months, buried 16 July 1861. (page 3)

Spence, Harriet Ann

B-78, Harriet Ann Spence, baptized 10 June 1860, daughter of James and Ann Spence. (page 10)

Spence, Harriet

B-214, Harriet Spence, baptized 6 March 1864, daughter of David and Catherine Spence of Poplar Point. (page 27)

Spence, Henry

B-170, Henry Spence, baptized 26 April 1863, son of Joseph and Janet Spence. (page 22)

Spence, Isabella

See James Johnston and Isabella Spence

Spence, James and Ann Whitford

M-9, James Spence, age 20, of Laprairie, son of Magnus Spence, married 6 September 1859, Ann Whitford, age 19, daughter of Peter Whitford, by William Cochran, Witnesses: Andrew Whitford and Francis Whitford. (page 5)

Spence, James

S-44, James Spence of Portage la Prairie, age 26 years, buried 9 December 1864. (page 6)

Spence, Jemima

B-208, Jemima Spence, baptized 14 February 1864, daughter of James and Ann Spence. (page 26)

Spence, Jemima

S-52, Jemima Spence of Portage la Prairie, age 2 years and 10 months, buried 5 May 1866. (page 7)

Spence, John

S-76, John Spence, of Portage la Prairie, age 70 years, buried 6 December 1869. (page 10)

Spence, Margaret

B-45, Margaret Spence, baptized 14 December 1858, daughter of Nicolas and Sophia Spence. (page 6)

Spence, Mary Anne

B-111, Mary Anne Spence, baptized 13 September 1861, daughter of David and Catherine Spence of Poplar Point. (page 14)

Spence, Mathew

B-135, Mathew Spence, baptized 27 April 1862, son of James and Anne Spence. (page 17)

Spence, Mathew

S-59, Mathew Spence of Portage la Prairie, age 7 months [?], buried 9 July 1867. (page 8)

Spence, Nancy

See Henry Monkman and Nancy Spence

Spence, Samuel and Catherine Moosoo

M-93, Samuel Spence (HB), age 32, of Sandy Bay, son of Baptiste Spence, married 30 December 1880, Catherine Moosoo, age 18, of Portage la Prairie, daughter of Bazile Moosoo, by Henry George, Witnesses: Joseph Sinclair and Victoria Favel. (page 47)

Spence, Sarah

S-8, Sarah Spence, of Portage la Prairie, age 39 years, buried 8 January 1858. (page 1)

Spence, Thomas Howard

B-538, Thomas Howard Spence, baptized 19 March 1882, son of Andrew and Letitia Spence of High Bluff. (page 68)

Spence, William

B-19, William Spence, baptized 10 August 1856, son of Nicol and Sophie Spence of Portage la Prairie. (page 3)

Spence, William James

B-513, William James Spence, born 24 March 1881, baptized 14 April 1881, son of Samuel and Catherine Spence of Sandy Bay Lake Manitoba. (page 65)

Strange, George

B-535, George Strange, born 4 November 1881, son of George and Elizabeth Strange (real estate Portage la Prairie). (page 67)

Stranger, Ann Harriet

B-177, Ann Harriet Stranger, baptized 28 June 1863, daughter of David and Eliza Stranger. (page 23)

Sturton, Edith Emily

B-574, Edith Emily Sturton, baptized 25 June 1883, daughter of Herbert and Adeline Sturton. (page 72)

Sutherland, William and Margaret Desjarlais

M-42, William Sutherland, age 20, of St. Marys, son of Robert Sutherland, married 27 June 1867, Margaret Desjaralis, age 20, daughter of Paul Desjarlais, by Henry George, Witnesses: Maria Henderson, Charles Anderson, Ann E. Hodgson, William G. Bird. (page 21)

Sutherland, William and Margaret Inkster

M-17, William Sutherland, age 26, of Red River, son of James Sutherland, married 21 October 1861, Margaret Inkster, of Red River, daughter of John Inkster, by, Thomas Cochrane, Witnesses: Gavin Garrioch and Peter Brown. (page 9)

Swanson, Kezia

B-203, Kezia Swanson, baptized 11 January 1864, daughter of James and Mary Ann Swanson. (page 26)

Tait, Benjamin

B-30, Benjamin Tait, baptized 24 May 1857, son of Joseph and Margaret Tait. (page 4)

Tait, Mary

S-14, Mary Tait, of Portage la Prairie, age 11 months, buried 21 June 1859. (page 2)

Tait, Mical

B-274, Michal Tait, baptized 2 September 1866, child of Joseph and Margaret Tait of Portage la Prairie. (page 35)

Tanner, Ann

B-33, Ann Tanner, baptized 2 Aug 1857, daughter of Edward Tanner and Indian. (page 5)

Tanner, John and Catherine Trottier

M-52, John Tanner, age 29, of St. Marys, son of James Tanner, married 14 July 1869, Catherine Sinclair, age _, widow, daughter of Joseph Trottier, by Henry George, Witnesses: James Tanner and John James Setter. (page 26)

Tanner, Margaret

See Baptiste Desmarais and Margaret Tanner

Tanner, Mary
> B-8, Mary Tanner, baptized 11 May 1856, daughter of Picito alias Tanner. (page 1)

Tanner, Samuel Baptiste
> S-9, Samuel Baptiste Tanner, of Portage la Prairie, age 8 months, buried 3 April 1858. (page 2)

Tanner, Thomas John
> B-7, Thomas John Tanner, baptized 11 May 1856, son of Picitoaha Tanner. (page 1)

Tate, Andrew and Eliza Anderson
> M-15, Andrew Tate, age 21, of Poplar Point, son of William Tate, married 7 February 1861, Eliza Anderson, age 16, of Laprairie, daughter of Thomas Anderson, by Thomas Cochrane, Witnesses: Mathew Cook and William Pocha. (page 8)

Tate, Ann Elizabeth
> B-194, Ann Elizabeth Tate, baptized 15 August 1867, _ and Mary Ann Tate. (page 37)

Tate, Catherine
> B-179, Catherine Tate, baptized 12 July 1863, daughter of Andrew and Eliza Tate. (page 23)

Tate, Catherine
> B-62, Catherine Tate, baptized 13 November 1859, daughter of James and Margaret Tate. (page 8)

Tate, Charles
> B-125, Charles Tate, baptized 19 January 1862, son of Andrew and Elizabeth Tate of Poplar Point. (page 16)

Tate, Elizabeth
> See Andrew West and Elizabeth Tate

Tate, Joseph William
> B-118, Joseph William Tate, baptized 13 December 1862, son of James and Margaret Tate of High Bluff. (page 15)

Tate, Margaret
> B-164, Margaret Tate, baptized 9 March 1863, daughter of James and Margaret Tate of High Bluff. (page 21)

Tate, Margaret
> S-31, Margaret Tate, of High Bluff, age 10 months, buried 5 February 1864. (page 4)

Tate, Maria

B-249, Maria Tate, baptized 27 August 1865, Andrew and Eliza Tate of Poplar Point. (page 32)

Tate, Mary Ann

See Charles Pocha and Mary Ann Tate

Tate, Mary Jane

B-197, Mary Jane Tate, baptized 6 December 1863, daughter of John and Catherine Tate of Poplar Point. (page 25)

Tate, Mary Jane

S-27, Mary Jane Tate of Poplar Point, age 1 month, buried 3 January 1864. (page 4)

Tate, Philip

B-93, Philip Tate, baptized 20 February 1861, son of John and Catherine Tate. (page 12)

Taylor, Eliza

B-192, Eliza Taylor, baptized 8 November 1863, son of Peter and Catherine Taylor. (page 24)

Taylor, Jane

B-221, Jane Taylor, baptized 13 April 1864, daughter of William and Margaret Taylor of Poplar Point. (page 28)

Taylor, Margaret

B-79, Margaret Taylor, baptized 2 August 1860, daughter of William and Margaret Taylor. (page 10)

Taylor, William

B-140, William Taylor, baptized 29 June 1862, son of William and Margaret Taylor of Poplar Point. (page 18)

Thompson, Lizzie

See Stewart Clark and Lizzie Thompson

Thompson, Maryetta

B-548, Maryette Thompson, born 16 December 1882, daughter of Stephen and Sara Thompson. (page 69)

Todd, Mary

See Joseph Kezinaugh Jr. and Mary Todd

Trottier, Catherine
>See John Tanner and Catherine Trottier

Turber, Ann
>S-98, Ann Turber, of Portage la Prairie, age 39 years, buried 14 November 1873. (page 13)

Turner, Elizabeth
>B-248, Elizabeth Margaret Turner, baptized 4 June 1865, daughter of Joseph and Jane Turner of Portage la Prairie. (page 31)

Turner, Joseph Alexander and Jane Whitford
>M-19, Joseph Alexander Turner, age 31, of Laprairie, son of Philip Turner, married 9 January 1862, Jane Whitford, age 16, daughter of Samuel Whitford, by Thomas Cochrane, Witnesses: Alexander Whitford and Alexander McBeth. (page 10)

Turner, Mary Jane
>B-168, Mary Jane Turner, baptized 12 April 1863, daughter of Joseph Alexander and Jane Turner. (page 21)

Vaughon, Amos Charles and Sarah Emma Blackburn
>M-91, Amos Charles Vaughon, age 37 of Selkirk, son of Amos H. Vaughon, married 3 December 1880, Sarah Emma Blackburn, age 28, of London, Ontario, daughter of Josiah Blackburn, by Henry George. (page 46)

Visnir, Ann Matilda Agnes
>B-512, Ann Matilda Agnes Visnir, baptized 12 February 1880, daughter of Isabella Visnir. (page 64)

Walker, Elizabeth Margaret
>S-91, Elizabeth Margaret Walker, of Portage la Prairie, age 12 years, buried 26 March 1873. (page 12)

Walker, Margaret
>See Wilder Bartlett and Margaret Walker

Wendle, Jane White
>See William Hamilton Garrioch and Jane White Wendle

West, Andrew and Elizabeth Tate
>M-95, Andrew West, age 23, of Winnipeg, son of Robert West, married 5 March 1881, Elizabeth Tate, age 19, of Winnipeg, daughter of John Tate, by Henry George. (page 48)

Whitford, Alexander and Elizabeth Jane Cook

M-49, Alexander Whitford, age 23, of St. Marys, son of Peter Whitford, married 19 March 1868, Elizabeth Jane Cook, age 16, of St. Margarets, daughter of Charles Cook, by Henry George, Witnesses: Elizabeth Adams and James Henderson. (page 25)

Whitford, Anabella

B-61, Anabella Whitford, baptized 25 September 1859, daughter of Samuel and Mary Whitford. (page 8)

Whitford, Andrew and Eliza Gill

M-14, Andrew Whitford, age 21, of Portage la Prairie, son of James Whitford, married 9 January 1861, Eliza Gill, age 16, of Portage la Prairie, by Thomas Cochran, Witnesses: David Taylor, Peter Henderson, and Joseph A. Turner. (page 7)

Whitford, Andrew

B-114, Andrew Whitford, baptized 6 October 1862, son of James and Mary Whitford. (page 15)

Whitford, Angus

B-107, Angus Whitford, baptized 25 August 1861, son of Simon and Maria Whitford. (page 14)

Whitford, Angus

S-30, Angus Whitford of Portage la Prairie, age 2 years and 6 months, buried 3 February 1864. (page 4)

Whitford, Ann

S-39, Ann Whitford of Portage la Prairie, age 12 years, buried 11 August 1864. (page 5)

Whitford, Ann

See James Spence and Ann Whitford

Whitford, Ann

See Andrew Spence and Ann Whitford

Whitford, Annaabelle

S-5, Annabelle Whitford, of Portage la Prairie, age 3 years, buried 23 June 1857. (page 1)

Whitford, Anne

B-130, Anne Whitford, baptized 2 Mar 1862, daughter of Francis and Jane Whitford. (page 17)

Whitford, Caroline

B-123, Caroline Whitford, baptized 12 January 1862, daughter of Samuel and Mary Whitford. (page 16)

Whitford, Catherine

B-285, Catherine Whitford, baptized 17 March 1867, daughter of James and Mary Whitford, La Prairie. (page 36)

Whitford, Catherine

S-63, Catherine Whitford, of Portage la Prairie, age 9 months, buried 28 January 1868. (page 8)

Whitford, Charles and Ann Anderson

Charles Whitford, age 21, of Portage la Prairie, son of Peter Whitford, married 2 December 1858, Ann Anderson, age 18, of Portage la Prairie, daughter fo Thomas Anderson, William Cochran, Witness: Henry LaRonde; Andrew Whitford. (page 2)

Whitford, Charles Thomas

B-4, Charles Thomas Whitford, baptized 20 January 1856, son of Simon and Maria Whitford of Portage la Prairie. (page 1)

Whitford, Christiana

See John Anderson and Christiana Whitford

Whitford, Colin

B-127, Colin Whitford, baptized 26 January 1862, son of Charles and Anne Whitford. (page 16)

Whitford, Elizabeth

B-364, Elizabeth Whitford, baptized 9 June 1871, daughter of Alexander and Elizabeth Jane Whitford of Laprairie. (page 45)

Whitford, Flora

B-80, Foral Whitford, baptized 5 September 1860, daughter of Charles and Nancy Whitford. (page 10)

Whitford, Francis and Jane Anderson

M-11, Francis Whitford, age 24, of Laprairie, son of James Whitford, married 29 September 1859, Jane Anderson, age 16, of Laprairie, daughter of Thomas Anderson, by William Cochran, Witnesses: Charles Whitford and Alexander Whitford. (page 6)

Whitford, George

    B-9, George Whitford, baptized 25 May 1856, son of Magnus and Mary Whitford of Laprairie. (page 2)

Whitford, George

    S-29, George Whitford of Portage la Prairie, age 5 years, buried 22 January 1864. (page 4)

Whitford, Henry Charles

    B-237, Henry Charles Whitford, baptized 22 January 1865, son of Charles and Ann Whitford of Laprairie. (page 30)

Whitford, Jane

    See Joseph Alexander Turner and Jane Whitford

Whitford, John Charles

    B-173, John Charles Whitford, baptized 10 May 1863, son of Magnus and Mary Whitford. (page 22)

Whitford, John Edmund

    B-167, John Edmund Whitford, baptized 5 April 1863, son of Charles and Ann Whitford. (page 21)

Whitford, Julia Mary

    B-188, Julia Mary Whitford, baptized 11 October 1863, daughter of Philip and Mary Whitford. (page 24)

Whitford, Lilly

    B-200, Lilly Whitford, baptized 27 December 1863, daughter of Francis and Jane Whitford. (page 25)

Whitford, Magnus and Mary Beads

    M-21, Magnus Whitford, of Laprairie, son of Peter Whitford, married 7 August 1862, Mary Beads, of Laprairie, daughter of John Beads, by William Cochrane, Witnesses: Henry Anderson and Maria Henderson. (page 21)

Whitford, Margaret

    B-77, Margaret Whitford, baptized 10 June 1860, daughter of Magnus and Sarah Spence. (page 10)

Whitford, Margaret

    B-77, Margaret Whitford, baptized 10 June 1860, daughter of Magnus and Sarah Spence. (page 10)

Whitford, Mary Jane
> B-501, Mary Jane Whitford, baptized 7 July 1880, daughter of William and Sarah Whitford. (page 63)

Whitford, Mary Matilda
> B-32, Mary Mathilde Whitford, baptized 2 August 1857, daughter of Samuel and Mary Whitford. (page 4)

Whitford, Mary
> S-62, Mary Whitford, of Portage la Prairie, age 28, buried 14 November 1867. (page 8)

Whitford, Peter Charles
> B-241, Peter Charles Whitford, baptized 7 May 1865, son of James and Mary Whitford of Laprairie. (page 31)

Whitford, Philip
> B-284, Philip Whitford, baptized 17 March 1867, son of Philip and Mary Whitford, La Prairie. (page 36)

Whitford, Sarah Ellen
> B-64, Sarah Ellen Whitford, baptized 27 November 1859, daughter of Simon and Maria Whitford. (page 8)

Whitford, Sarah
> S-19, Sarah Spence, of Portage la Prairie, age __, wife of Magnus Whitford, buried 24 December 1861. (page 3)

Whitford, Simon
> B-202, Simon Whitford, baptized 7 January 1864, son of James and Mary Whitford. (page 26)

Whitford, Simon
> S-33, Simon Whitford of Portage la Prairie, age 2-1/2 months, buried 12 March 1864. (page 5)

Whitford, Thomas William
> B-184, Thomas William Whitford, baptized 4 October 1863, son of Andrew and Eliza Whitford. (page 23)

Whitford, William
> B-41, William Whitford, baptized 23 May 1858, son of Magnus and Sarah Whitford. (page 6)

Whitford, William

S-13, William Whitford, of Portage la Prairie, age 1 year, buried 28 May 1859. (page 2)

Whitised, T.

S-179, T. Whitised, of Portage la Prairie, age __, buried 28 November 1881. (page 23)

Wishart, Margaret Jane

B-216, Margaret Jane Wishart, baptized 7 March 1864, daughter of James and Eliza Wishart of Poplar Point. (page 27)

Wishart, Robert and Clementine McLean

M-69, Robert Wishart, age 25, of Portage la Prairie, son of John Wishart, married 9 December 1872, Clementine McLean, age 21, of Portage la Prairie, daughter of John McLean, by Henry George, Witness: Alexander Cameron. (page 35)

Wray, Adeline Flora

B-212, Adeline Flora Wray, baptized 25 February 1864, daughter of William Finley and Frances Wray of High Bluff. (page 27)

Wray, J. Finley and Frances Desmarais

M-26, J. Finlay Wray, of Poplar Bluff, married 30 April 1863, Frances Desmarais, of Poplar Bluff, daughter of Baptiste Desmarais, by William Cochran, Witnesses: Andrew Peterson and Joseph Adams. (page 13)

Young, Elizabeth R.

B-500, Elizabeth R. Young, bt. 17 June 1880, daughter of John B. and Ellen Young, Wellington P. O. (page 63)

Young, Isabella

B-477, Isabella Young, baptized 14 April 1879, daughter of John B. and Ellen Young, Wellington P. O. (page 60)

..., Ann (adopted)

B-196, Ann ..., baptized 29 November 1868, daughter of John and Mary .. [probably Norquay]of High Bluff. (page 25)

www.ingramcontent.com/pod-product-compliance
Lightning Source LLC
Chambersburg PA
CBHW081845280526
45789CB00007B/2570